Praise for

Tales of a Prison Psychiatrist

FIFTY YEARS OF CRIMINALIZATION OF THE MENTALLY ILL AND ADDICTED

—————

"Dr. Kaufman's powerful book casts a hopeful light on a critical issue of our time: the seemingly intractable problem of mentally ill and addicted patients caught up in our nation's prison system.

"His compelling and deftly written memoir weaves together Kaufman's depth of knowledge and the stories of real lives. He offers solutions based on hard-won insights, a perspective gleaned over the decades both as a psychiatrist and as an expert witness.

"This book should be required reading for those who could make a difference in the areas of prisons, mental health, and addiction – which is to say, in the future of our nation."

– Allene Symons, *Aldous Huxley's Hands: His Quest for Perception and the Origin and Return of Psychedelic Science*

"A spectacular insight into our prison situation beautifully written by a lifetime authority on the subject."

– Julie Brickman, *Two Deserts* & *What Birds Can Only Whisper*,
Fiction faculty, MFA in Writing, Spalding University

Dr. Ed Kaufman takes us into the world of the mentally ill and addicted as it was, as it is now, and as he hopes it will be. Based on his personal experiences as a Psychiatric doctor...and as he reveals specific incidents...it is difficult to read. But what gives the reader hope is the successful alternative treatments Dr. Kaufman has worked so hard to implement into our present system.

– Janet Simcic, *The Man at the Caffe' Farnese*,
The Man at the Rialto Bridge,
The Man at the Spanish Steps, and *An American Chick's Guide to Italy*

Tales of a Prison Psychiatrist

FIFTY YEARS OF CRIMINALIZATION OF THE MENTALLY ILL AND ADDICTED

to John .
my fellow author
in the cause

Dr. Edward Kaufman

Gray Matter Imprints, Irvine, California

GRAY MATTER IMPRINT EDITION

ISBN: 0986285374

ISBN 13: 9780986285370

Library of Congress Control Number 2017901563.

Gray Matter Consultants LLC,Laguna Woods, CALIFORNIA

Kaufman, Edward, MD

TALES OF A PRISON PSYCHOLOGIST: Fifty Years of Criminalization of the Mentally Ill and Addicted ISBN-13: 978-0986285370 (Gray Matter Consultants LLC). ISBN-10: 0986285374.

1. Mental Illness. 2. Addiction. 3. Criminalization. 4. Brutalization. 5. Role of Judges.

Cover design and typesetting is by Rena Konheim, RBSafran Design. Cover photo shows a group therapy session from within the California State Prison System.

Published and printed in the United States of America by Gray Matter Imprints, the publishing division of Gray Matter Consultants LLC, PO Box 50278, Irvine, CA 92619.

10 9 8 7 6 5 4 3 2 1

Gray Matter accepts queries only.at:

Gray Matter Imprints

P.O. Box 50278

Irvine, CA 92619

Email: *imprints@gray-matter.us*

Table of Contents

Acknowledgements

FIRST AND FOREMOST, I WOULD like to acknowledge my wife, Karen Redding, who has always encouraged me to stay fresh and move ahead, yet stay in the moment of observation and reflection.

Many early mentors stand out in the field of psychiatry, notably Lawrence C. Kolb, Alvin Mesnikoff and Stanley Lessor. My early influences in the treatment of addictive disorders included Vincent Dole, Pauline Kaufmann and Mitch Rosenthal. Seymour Halleck supported me in staying with my work in jails and prisons. Michael Bien tirelessly continued the Coleman suit for over 20 years to facilitate improved mental health care and overcrowding in all California state prisons.

I would also like to thank my creative writing mentors at Antioch University's creative writing program, most notably Steve Heller and David Ulin for their mentorship and dedication to social justice.

Lastly, I could not have written this book without the support of my writing groups, which included Julie Brickman, Susan Dworkin, Janet Simcic, Brenda Barrie and the always helpful Allene Symons.

Dedication

This book is dedicated to
the freedom of all the
mentally ill and addicted persons
who are wrongly incarcerated
in the USA.

Prologue

———

FEBRUARY 2013. A CALIFORNIA STATE prison

A cell extraction is about to begin. Dr. M, a psychiatrist in a stab-proof vest, approaches a door at the end of a cellblock. With more frustration than compassion, he attempts to cajole an inmate into putting handcuffs on and leaving his locked cell. He obviously has no rapport with the inmate, whom I will call John.

John, anticipating what is about to happen, pleads, "Don't treat me like a dog!" After less than a minute, the psychiatrist gives up and steps aside.

The hallway fills with eight guards, each in full protective gear: helmet; gas mask; clear, plastic-covered Hazmat suit; and flak vest. At their belts are expandable batons and grenades of pepper spray. Each guard barks out his name for the video.

Finding an opening in the door jam, a guard squirts three quick shots of pepper spray into the cell.

John screams, "You're going to screw me!" He then begs to see the psychiatrist.

Off to one side, the psychiatrist remains impassive. A guard yells, "You missed your chance for that. Face the back wall. Back up and place both hands through the food port." Handcuffs are readied.

"You're going to fuck me up the ass!"

The guards try another tack. "Strip and come out!" Another shot of spray.

"You want to screw me," screams John. "I'm not a homosexual."

In response to John's paranoia, the guards haul in a long-nosed "cell buster" and jam the nozzle into the food port, unaware they are actualizing John's worst fears. John screams with pain when the seventh blast of pepper spray overcomes him. Even the cameraman on his distant perch coughs repeatedly, jerking the video camera and image back and forth.

The guards unlock the cell door, overwhelm John and pin him against the back wall with their heavy stun shields. They strip his remaining underwear and cuff his ankles and wrists. The guards shout more orders. "Show us your hands!" "Open your mouth!" "Lift up your testicles!" They fear hidden weapons.

As they exit the cell, John and his handlers slip and fall in a flow of urine and feces that is streaming out of the doorway.

John, stark naked, is forced to lie on a gurney. He is strapped down on his back, his genitals exposed, and rolled down the hall in full sight of other inmates.

Muffled by a spit mask, John makes one last attempt to be treated fairly: "I'm OK. I won't give you a problem."

I am watching a video of a year-old event, but even so, I feel nauseated.

In the days following this extraction, John was brought before a review committee on a charge of "obstructing a peace officer in the line of duty." He received an extended jail term of sixty days, depriving him of earned "good time" despite a mental-health evaluation that his diagnosis, schizophrenia, led to his aberrant behavior. He was also deprived of all social contact for a month after leaving the prison mental-health unit.

I watched this video repeatedly, as it was part of my review and assessment of mental-health care, including use of force, in the California state prison system.

This was my second call to do so in twenty years. The video bore witness to the system's management of a psychotic, fecal-smearing inmate, using a "planned" correctional cell extraction. The more frequently used "immediate use of force" extraction was never recorded. "Immediate use of force" is California correctional extraction at its best, justified by the California

Department of Corrections and Rehabilitation according to its book of regulations. I can't imagine how the spontaneous use of force could be worse than planned use of force, but it must be horrendous.

My request to watch the recording on my own was granted only after a protracted argument between the state's attorney, who insisted on being present during the viewing, and the inmate's representative. In the 1990s, when Tasers and rubber pellet guns were introduced to control disturbed inmates, I thought these methods symptomatic of a lack of effective treatment. While this video demonstrated how less lethal methods had replaced these weapons, the underlying mentality condoning brutality nonetheless remained.

I interviewed John a few days after I watched the extraction videotape.

Pepper spray, he said, was "suffocating . . . taking all the oxygen away that belongs inside you; it chokes you out, it takes the life out of you." After a pause, and a few words of encouragement from me, he continued. "It burns your skin . . . I feel like my skin is going to fall off."

John felt fear whenever the extraction team approached. "When they're all geared up, it feels like they're coming in to kill me. When they come into the cell, they hold you up against the wall with a shield, so you can't move."

John described a total fear of custody staff, the result of many past "beat-downs" with pepper spray. He had frequent nightmares in which he was jumped on and beaten by guards. He told me he took his medications only because he was afraid they'd beat him if he didn't.

He preferred never to leave his cell so he could minimize interactions with guards and other custodial staff. This increased John's isolation, and his hesitancy to receive therapy outside of his cell further contributed to the deterioration of his mental health.

I assessed three other inmates who had been subjected to extractions. Like John, they all had early histories of drug addiction now dwarfed by mental illness after years of incarceration. They, too, were brought before a review committee for "obstructing a peace officer in the line of duty." Their jail terms were all extended by sixty to ninety days despite mental-health evaluations stating that their mental illnesses led to their aberrant behavior. I reviewed the charts of dozens of other inmates who were subjected to use of force. In every case, inmates were punished for their psychotic behavior by depriving them of "good time."

In my mind—and in the words of the federal judge who tried this case— bringing punitive measures against John and the other inmates for their psychotic behavior is nothing short of inhumane. I remain puzzled as to which is the more egregious: the brutal, physically and psychologically damaging extractions or punishing the victims for being too frightened and psychotic to leave their cells by extending their prison stays and depriving them of human contact during solitary confinement and for months thereafter.

The Origins of Criminalization

CHAPTER 1

Criminalization of the Mentally Ill and Addicted

———

I HAVE BEEN WITNESS TO the past five decades of criminalization of the mentally ill and addicted in the United States. Each phase of this mistreatment evolved despite the good intentions of many individuals who founded and developed these movements. In the mid-nineteenth century, Dorothea Dix freed the mentally ill from prisons and helped develop over 30 psychiatric hospitals with the goal of providing humane care for the mentally ill. My first visit to a state psychiatric hospital was during my junior year of medical school in 1958. Even my inexperienced eye could tell care was lacking by then. I witnessed the deterioration of state psychiatric hospitals shortly after I began my psychiatric training in 1961 at Columbia University's New York State Psychiatric Institute, or PI, as it was called then. PI was part of the state system and a richly funded institution, but the university required all three-year psychiatry residents to pay their dues by spending two months at Rockland State Psychiatric Hospital.

My fellow residents and I dreaded the time away from our prestigious training program, viewing our stay at Rockland as a form of servitude in Bedlam. Columbia made the experience bearable by offering, only at the state hospital, interesting courses not on the basic curriculum. Years later I still remember my literal and metaphorical take-away from one of these classes: the therapist's chair should not be any more comfortable than the patient's. Although almost never practiced at Rockland State, the concept that patient and therapist are in parallel hierarchies was and still is an important lesson for me.

Interpersonality was a necessary lesson in those days of Freudian authoritarian psychiatry, though it is championed by many systems of therapy today. I wasn't aware of it at the time, but my observations of the conditions at that state hospital introduced me to this system just as these institutions were phasing down and beginning to lead us to criminalization of the mentally ill.

Simeon Chlenoff, the director of Rockland, invited me to join him on his daily rounds. As we walked the expansive, manicured hospital grounds, he gestured toward the patients who were caretakers of his house and garden. He beamed when he said they were like part of his family, content as they were doing their assigned jobs. As they cleaned his house, mowed his lawn, and trimmed his hedges, they reminded me of slaves on a plantation.

Chlenoff said he often made rounds in the middle of the night because, "That's the time when the staff beat the patients. The staff never knows when I am coming. This is the only way I can stop them from slamming them."

Chlenoff's tutoring and my experiences running a ward at Rockland helped me compare the problems of a state hospital with those in jails and prisons when I began my work there a few years later.

Ken Kesey's book, *One Flew over the Cuckoo's Nest*, was published in 1962, the same year as my rotation at Rockland State. The book did much to bring public awareness to the often sadistic and barbaric treatment in the psychiatric hospitals of the day. Even at advanced therapeutic institutions like the Psychiatric Institute, we were still performing an occasional lobotomy. I administered electric shock therapy (ECT) under conditions only a bit more humane than those depicted in the 1975 movie version of Kesey's book. Today ECT is safer and more effective than it was in the '60s,

Psychiatric Institute was research-oriented, and in my second year there, I began doing sleep research with Dr. Howard Roffwarg. He helped me examine two issues relevant to my emerging interest in the field of addiction.

In the first study we determined that a small dose of LSD would greatly drive the amount of dreaming time in the first few hours of sleep. The second helped launch my involvement in the clinical aspects of substance abuse. This was a study of the effects of heroin withdrawal on sleep. No one on the faculty of Columbia had the slightest idea how to detoxify a heroin addict.

I finally found a psychiatrist, Dr. Lonnie McDonald, who worked in Harlem and taught me how to perform a relatively painless withdrawal. I did panic at times because the symptoms were difficult to evaluate, but eventually we succeeded. I stayed up all night with the addicted patient, monitoring the then-primitive brain wave recording device to be sure pens didn't stick or run out of ink.

Our published findings substantiated an already obvious clinical fact: sleep is grossly disturbed when detoxifying from heroin or other opiates. I quickly became labeled an addiction expert because of a genuine lack of knowledge about drug and alcohol misuse among most New York City psychiatrists at the time. A few years later I became editor in chief of the *American Journal of Drug and Alcohol Abuse*, a position I held for the next 35 years.

It is not surprising that no one at PI knew how to detoxify a heroin addict in 1963. At that time it was illegal to treat an addict outside of a hospital setting. Doctors who did so in their private offices faced criminal charges, and many physicians had been punished for doing so. Outpatient methadone maintenance treatment was introduced a year later. It was not approved by the FDA as a treatment for heroin addiction until 1972, and then only in specially supervised programs.

My brief time in a state hospital helped qualify me as an expert in this field, and in the 1970s, I was called upon to evaluate the quality of psychiatric care in legal suits filed against five state hospitals outside of New York. My evaluation was ultimately published in *The American Journal of Psychiatry* in 1979.

Taken together, the problems I observed at these five institutions illustrate many of the reasons these hospitals have been phased out. Two of these were in Texas. The first had an adequate physical plant but no psychiatrist providing clinical services, only MDs trained in other specialties. This resulted in gross overmedication without proper monitoring of serious side effects, leading to a ward full of slobbering, zombie-like patients. Seclusion was used as punishment rather than containment, ECT was done without proper assessment and safeguards, and no individualized treatment was provided.

The second hospital was larger, dreary, and provided no personal privacy. Drugs were used inappropriately and seclusion punitively. There were psychiatrists here, but only a fourth of the number suggested by emerging national standards, which mandated that an involuntary patient had a constitutional right to adequate treatment.

The third hospital was in Ohio and used a form of reality therapy, which truly was cruel and unusual punishment. Every patient was placed in seclusion immediately after being admitted. Following this isolation, all potentially problematic clients were secured to their bed by cuffing hands and legs, and using leather waist belts. The cuffs were released briefly so patients could perform simple tasks like making their beds and rolling up their toilet paper. When they were able to do these well, they were permitted 30 minutes in a sparse dayroom with other patients.

If they did not attack the other patients and continued their basic assignments, they would be considered for transfer to a less-structured environment. It took patients 60 to 90 days to qualify to leave this unit. Some of them became so dependent on wrist cuffs to control their impulses they couldn't stop hitting others when their hands were not secured. All the psychiatrists and psychologists but one left these wards because of the inhumanity of this so-called treatment. The remaining doctor just signed all the orders for seclusion and restraints as long as "they were in line."

The fourth hospital housed more than a thousand patients in a northeastern state. None of the psychiatrists was board-certified, and each had a caseload of 100 to 200 patients. Individual and group therapy were almost nonexistent. The majority of patients were maintained for the duration of their hospital stay on the same dose of meds they were placed on the day they were admitted. I found this shocking, as medication for new, involuntarily hospitalized patients should be reviewed at least several times weekly and, invariably, needs to be modified regularly to weigh therapeutic efficacy against side effects.

The fifth state psychiatric hospital I evaluated was in Utah. Here I was asked to assess a therapeutic community form of treatment on a maximum-security unit. A therapeutic milieu was created on this ward where patients assumed responsibility for themselves. When they learned to do so, they were assigned to team up with and be helpful to sicker clients. The mentors were held responsible when their mentees became sicker. This form of treatment, which I also had utilized in similar settings, worked quite well. Psychotic behavior was controlled and reversed without the use of physical restraints or high doses of injectable or oral psychiatric meds. However, I learned that budget cuts and removal of the hospital superintendent who implemented this program were threatening to undermine it.

I returned here for a second evaluation three months later. The treatment environment was already severely compromised by budgetary restrictions and lack of administrative support. The number of intramuscular injections of Thorazine, a powerful antipsychotic medication with many side effects, was rapidly increasing. So too were oral doses of other powerful medications to control symptoms. The ward was threatened with closure by the new hospital administration at the time of my reevaluation. Interestingly, it was the availability of Thorazine for Schizophrenia in 1954 that was instrumental in leading to the erroneous belief that state psychiatric hospitals could be phased out.

None of the five hospitals I evaluated met the federal standard of care mandated by a 1972 law intended to remedy the problems at these institutions. As a result of the suit invoking this law, several inhumane practices were banned, and more mental health staff were hired at many state hospitals. Overall, however, these changes did not stem the tide that was closing these hospitals and turning the patients loose.

My assessments of these hospitals, several other psychiatric facilities I had observed, and my own experiences at Rockland State confirmed my growing conviction that this system of care of the severely ill was dysfunctional and had to change. It was changing; but it was self-destructing rapidly. I never dreamed then that what would replace the state psychiatric hospital would be far worse than anything I could imagine.

I was part of the beginning of deinstitutionalization and the birth of community psychiatry during my residency at Columbia University's State Psychiatric Institute in 1963. I had high hopes this movement would replace and revolutionize the fading dysfunctional state psychiatric systems. This deinstitutionalization was not well planned or adequately funded. Over half of planned community mental health centers were never built. This lack of foresight led to trans-institutionalization of the mentally ill to jails and prisons in a manner that made the state hospitals look like luxury resorts. As community funds dried up, more and more psychiatric patients and addicts roamed the streets of our cities, living in the squalor of homelessness without support or mental-health care, consequently making them increasingly vulnerable to incarceration.

I learned firsthand about mental-health patients in prison when I was hired as a psychiatrist at the Lewisburg Federal Penitentiary in Pennsylvania in 1964. While there, I attempted to develop humane treatment for mentally ill inmates and to educate a handful of guards about how human behavior often comes in shades of gray.

Now, when I compare my memory of Lewisburg to other prison systems, it was one of the better correctional facilities I have seen. Perhaps my tenure there looked rosy because it was my first prison job. It was recently named by liberal publication *Mother Jones* as one of the ten worst prisons in the United States. Lewisburg is now home to a special management unit, which holds prisoners in locked down, two-person cells almost constantly. This is long-term isolation, considered ineffective and psychologically damaging, a point this book is intended to emphasize.

I played tennis with the warden at Lewisburg on a weekly basis, but he enjoyed playing other games with me. He knew I considered solitary confinement, or "the Hole," cruel and unusual punishment and was universally opposed to it. When I first served on the prison disciplinary committee, I would vote against any time in solitary for almost every infraction. The warden would then not count my vote at all, depending instead on the average of the two custodial members of the committee for his decision.

However, if I voted for a single day in the Hole, my vote was averaged in, and the inmate would spend one-third less time in punitive segregation. For the ultimate welfare of the inmates, I began voting for one day in solitary. The warden won that game, and I could only retaliate with overhead smashes at the tennis net, directed at his mid-section—or lower, if I could get away with it.

I'd accepted this position at Lewisburg as an alternative to serving in Vietnam. Several conscientious objectors were among my patients. I was conflicted when called upon to deal with a hunger strike by an objector who, as a vegan, had refused to wear a leather belt and shoes. His hair fell below his shoulders, and his beard was as full as mine was before I was required to shave it to work at the federal prison. I had also stopped eating meat by then. He was a college graduate and I felt a greater commonality with him than with the guards.

I worked out a compromise with him and prison authorities about his belt and shoes, and somehow convinced him to resume eating and not seriously endanger his life. I would have been in great conflict if force-feeding—which had been seriously considered—had been utilized. I was greatly relieved the problem was resolved without it.

In 1966, upon completion of my two-year stint as chief of psychiatric services at Lewisburg, I felt honored when offered the position of attending psychiatrist of the community service at Columbia University's Psychiatric Institute [PI].

Community psychiatry was in its heyday at that time. A separate Department of Community Psychiatry was formed to train fellows in this field, and a new *Journal of Hospital and Community Psychiatry* was published for the first time. The research-oriented department at PI opened a community psychiatric in-patient program to treat the mentally disturbed patients who lived in the Washington Heights area of Manhattan. Given that the hospital previously catered to privileged families, this new unit was revolutionary. Some of the prior research interests of the faculty at that time were schizophrenic twins, idiot savants, nascent sleep research, borderline personalities (or "pseudoneurotic" schizophrenics, as they were then called at PI), along with development of the DSM-III (Diagnostic and Statistical Manual), which became the bible of psychiatric diagnoses until DSM-IV was published in 1994. DSM-5 was released in 2015.

I replaced Dr. John Talbott as attending psychiatrist on this community unit after he left to fulfill his military obligation in Vietnam. He later went on to be editor in chief of the *Journal of Hospital and Community Psychiatry.*

My chief resident was Dr. Dick Elpers, who become chief of mental health for Orange County, California, and eventually helped lure me away from New York. PI was an exciting place to be in the late '60s. The staff was young, bright, and sincere in their desire to help their patients, and innovative but experienced supervisors guided us.

John F. Kennedy was inspiring and well-meaning when on February 5, 1963, he addressed Congress on mental health and retardation, proposing a new program where the federal government would fund Community Mental Health Centers (CMHCs) to replace the state hospitals. Kennedy called the state hospitals "shamefully understaffed, overcrowded, unpleasant institutions from which death provided the only firm hope of release." He and his advisors idealistically envisioned that ". . . reliance on the cold mercy of custodial isolations will be supplanted by the open warmth of community concern and capability." [Torrey, E. Fuller. 2014]

One motivation behind Jack Kennedy's creating the CMHCs was to honor his sister, Rosemary, who was institutionalized most of her life with mental retardation and mental illness. Suffering from uncontrollable rages, she received a lobotomy in 1941 that led to additional severe brain damage. Kennedy made a great effort to enhance recognition and treatment for individuals like his sister, who at the time were classified as "retarded" rather than the kinder term used today, intellectually disabled.

Kennedy listed certain criteria to receive funding for a CMHC. One of the criteria was inpatient services for a catchment area, the region from which an institution's population is drawn. Such a service was created at Psychiatric Institute in part to meet this requirement. I was excited not just to have a job but also to participate in this new movement to provide warm, compassionate treatment meant to end the woes of the chronic mentally ill. I hoped to help this program adapt to treating a potpourri of patients, including ex-felons and potentially violent, previously untreated individuals. By now, I was looking forward to treating difficult mental patients outside of correctional facilities.

Years later, E. Fuller Torrey succinctly summarized why the community mental health movement failed in his comprehensive book, *American Psychosis*. The CMHC "encouraged the closing of state mental hospitals without any realistic plan regarding what would happen to the discharged patients, especially those who refused to take the medication they needed to stay well. It included no plan for the future funding of the mental health centers. . . By bypassing the states it guaranteed that future services would not be coordinated."

Twenty-two days after the bill was signed on October 31, 1963, Kennedy was assassinated. Torrey quoted Alonzo Hamby, who said the Kennedy legislative program was funded "as a memorial to a national martyr."

President Lyndon Johnson shifted Kennedy's emphasis on repair of juvenile justice to a war on crime and began the militarization of local police forces, which went relatively unnoticed until recent years and led to increasing prison populations. Mass imprisonment of addicts also led to prison and jail overcrowding, which hampered the treatment of the mentally ill as well as of the addicted, many of whom were themselves also mentally ill [35 percent by most estimates].

President Richard Nixon so intensely disliked community mental health that he repeatedly tried to defund the program. Many conservative politicians linked mental health to communism in the 1960s. I even feared I'd be labeled another "commie" psychiatrist for my own political views at the time. Only six percent of psychiatrists/psychoanalysts voted for Nixon in 1968.

Many CMHCs were encouraged to become socially and politically active, feeding still further into Nixon's dislike of mental health. In the eight years following Nixon's taking office, the state hospital census declined by another 230,000. He repeatedly recommended terminating the CMHC programs, but a Democratic Congress kept restoring the budget cuts to keep it functioning. Nixon also declared a war on drugs in 1971, enacting mandatory sentencing, including classifying marijuana with the most dangerous of drugs, a major step toward mass incarceration.

In 1970, social protesters turned against an important CMHC at Lincoln Hospital in the Bronx, occupying and damaging the local program, and contributing to the demise of the national movement. A similar protest staged at St. Luke's Hospital in Manhattan demanded comprehensive treatment for drug addiction. I was then director of emergency psychiatric services at St. Luke's, and I knew many of the activists. They were aware I had goals similar to their own, but they continued to occupy the ER until more treatment for addicts became available.

Homelessness was a taboo in New York at that time, and we were able to find city-funded lodging for almost every homeless person who came to the ER. Unfortunately, we often had to resort to rundown, overpriced, single-room-occupancy hotels, which were barely better than being on the streets. Until recently, there were few solution-seeking protests concerning the mushrooming hordes of mentally ill, arrest-prone homeless people who flooded our streets.

I still vividly recall my first and only emergency home visit during the time I worked in the ER at St. Luke's Hospital. Members of a local police team asked me to join them on a domestic violence call where the husband suffered from a manic-depressive disorder. They showed me how they handled these problems rather than await my advice. They approached the patient and, before there were any introductions, punched him full force in the abdomen, immobilizing and cuffing him before I said a word. I have heard that today's mental health ride-alongs, which have recently become more common, are more collaborative.

Shortly before President Jimmy Carter lost his reelection bid to Ronald Reagan in 1980, he signed an act that continued the CHMC, finally with more state involvement.

Reagan, who had deinstitutionalized mental-health patients in California while serving as governor, quickly nationalized the decimation of mental-health care. He discarded the Community Mental Health Act and redirected the funds as block grants to the states, leaving the states free to allocate monies to highways, bridges and anything but care of the mentally ill.

This was the final death knell for community mental health.

Reagan's Comprehensive Crime Control Act of 1984 eliminated the federal parole system; emphasized interdiction of drug imports; and neglected prevention, treatment and research. (Except for Nancy Reagan's limited "just say no" campaign).

Political conservatives in the Reagan era joined civil rights attorneys in emptying state hospitals still further, despite their differing priorities. Liberal attorneys prioritized personal freedom to refuse medication and involuntary hospitalization over curing or stemming their clients' mental illness. Both factions shared seemingly total disregard for the fact that there were progressively fewer community resources to manage these patients. This alliance foreshadowed the political right and left coming together again in 2014 to support Prop 47 and begin to reverse mass incarceration, which had been so instrumental in criminalizing the mentally ill for 50 years.

The Anti-Drug Abuse Act of 1986 made the penalty for possession of five grams of crack cocaine, favored by African-Americans, equivalent to penalties for 500 grams of powder, then favored by whites. A mandatory prison sentence of five years was imposed on convicted defendants, a substantial factor in the mass incarcerations of African-Americans.

In 1987, Reagan escalated the war on drugs, leading to an eightfold increase in the number of people—400,000—incarcerated for nonviolent drug crimes in the first seven years of his presidency. This continuing war was a major factor in escalating mass incarcerations and did little to stem the tide of addiction.

George H.W. Bush actualized Lyndon Johnson's war on drugs with militarization of drug abuse enforcement. Heavily armed SWAT teams conducted 40,000 drug raids annually during his administration, mostly for nonviolent drug crimes.

Ironically, two months after Reagan became president, he was shot by John Hinckley, a young man with schizophrenia. Although Reagan attempted to visit Hinckley, reportedly in an attempt to forgive him, the president never showed any interest in funding mental health. Thirty-four years later, in 2016, the controversy over Hinckley's release from a federal psychiatric hospital ended with his full discharge in August 2016. Hinckley had spent only 13 days a month in St. Elizabeth's Hospital in Washington, DC from 2013 till his release and the rest with his 89-year-old mother in Virginia, where he lived full time upon his discharge.

Decreased funding for mental health continued even during the terms of liberal presidents who followed Reagan. During Democrat Barack Obama's administration, states cut mental-health expenditures by $5 billion between 2009 and 2012, and eliminated 4,500 public psychiatric beds. The economic recession of that time helped fuel the diminishing monies for mental-health and other social programs.

Involuntary hospitalization laws became even more restrictive. Medicare and Medicaid excluded funding for mental patients in any psychiatric hospital with more than 16 beds, only funding mental health care after they were discharged. This paved the way for even more of the severely mentally ill to leave hospitals and enter neighborhoods where there were few treatment facilities, no housing, few if any hospital beds, and little capacity for involuntary treatment. Thousands were housed in board and care homes that were often more wretched than state hospitals. Mentally ill individuals steadily filled jails and prisons, already overflowing because of punitive sentencing policies like the three-strikes law, and harsher sentences for drug-related crimes and probation violations.

Liberal presidents also contributed to mass incarceration. Bill Clinton's version of the war on drugs resulted in an increase of 673,000 inmates in the total prison population, far more than during Reagan's tenure.

Psychiatric patients continue to suffer the most in overcrowded penal environments. Their fear of prison guards and other inmates escalates. They are unable to understand and follow guidelines, are housed in secure areas that deprive them of needed human contact, and are punished severely for their psychotic behaviors. When they are finally released, it is to inadequate housing, treatment, and aftercare programs—if any—resulting in rapid recidivism.

A survey released in 2014 by the Treatment Advocacy Center, to which forty-nine states and the District of Columbia responded, confirmed my impression that the problem was nationwide. Torrey and his associates at the center concluded: "The number of individuals with serious mental illness in prisons and jails throughout the USA now exceeds the number in state psychiatric hospitals tenfold."

Following my stint in Lewisburg, I'd had nightmares in which I was again drafted to work in a federal prison. These dreams of involuntary servitude reinforced my strong desire to never again work in a penal institution.

However, in 1970, political upheaval drew me back. A series of riots took place in the Attica Correctional Facility and in several New York City jails, including the infamous Tombs in lower Manhattan. Stones from an earlier version built in 1735 were used to build the Tombs one hundred years later. The design of the

Tombs came from an ancient Egyptian mausoleum. The basic architecture and recycled stones used to build this jail made it appear as though it had been built in the eighteenth century. The inside structure was as inadequate as the façade. At the time of the upheaval, the Tombs housed more than double its capacity, and suicide was rampant.

As a result of public outcry about these conditions, the budget for prison mental health was increased greatly, and the search was on for a chief. Even though I was only in my early thirties, I accepted the position of director of mental health for the entire New York City system, which then and now processes 100,000 admissions yearly. I was surprised to be offered this responsible position at such a young age. The offer came about as a result of my experience at Lewisburg as well as my politics fitting in with those of John Lindsay, at the time the liberal Republican mayor of New York City.

After I left the city position, I became medical director of a large addiction treatment program on New York City's multiethnic Lower East Side, where I implemented family therapy and other programs to treat addiction and help opiate addicts get off of methadone maintenance safely. This program also had a special component to treat elderly Chinese addicts who had been addicted to opium in China or became addicted to heroin by sweatshop operators who victimized them. Treatment for this group of addicted persons was totally different from that of other addicts and began to teach me the need for culturally based variations in treatment.

State psychiatric hospitals still handled the vast majority of the severely mentally ill in 1971. The psychiatric population in New York City jails in 1971 was estimated at only five percent of the total. It has since increased at least fivefold. Mental illness was much more common in women inmates then, a finding that continues to this day in most correctional systems.

As of early 2014, the rate of psychiatric illness in California prisons was twenty-eight percent, with 33,250 mentally ill inmates. The federal order to lower the state prison census led, in part, to 3,200 psychiatric patients in L.A. County jails. (In general, federal and state correctional facilities are called prisons, and city and county institutions are referred to as jails). The L.A. County jail system is commonly referred to as the world's largest psychiatric hospital. L.A.'s major competitor for this title, Cook County Jail in Chicago, found that 3,500 —or one-third of inmates—were seriously mentally ill. In 2015, this jail decided to appoint a psychologist as warden to deal with the problem of so many mentally ill inmates.

The Bureau of Justice estimated in 2015 that over fifty-six percent of state offenders have mental-health problems, and more than one million mentally ill individuals are presently incarcerated in the United States. Most other estimates are closer to a range of 25 percent and 350,000 to 500,000 individuals. When these sick patients are discharged from state prisons and local jails—untreated and without adequate resources, housing or aftercare—they quickly relapse and return to custody.

Six percent to ten percent of the adult population of this country suffers from schizophrenia, bipolar disorder or severe depression, leaving them vulnerable to the correctional system. Twenty-five million Americans over the age of twelve use illicit drugs. Almost any one of us can end up in jail. All it takes is an extra drink, tranquilizer or pain med, a traffic stop or an angry or suicidal threat. Everyone I speak with who has been incarcerated, even for a few hours, is traumatized by the experience. Mentally disturbed individuals are extremely difficult to manage in jails and prisons. They exhibit major behavioral problems; are more often abused, beaten and/or raped; become sicker during incarceration; spend more time in segregation and incarceration; and commit suicide more often. They are more costly than other inmates and are repeatedly re-incarcerated. [Torrey, *American Psychosis*, 2014]

According to a 2014 study published in the *American Journal of Public Health*, half of those who are on medication for a mental-health condition do not get their medication after they are imprisoned, another example of how poorly correctional systems handle the mentally ill. I'm often frustrated by how difficult—if not impossible—it is to keep my patients on their meds when they enter Orange County, California, jails.

In the New York City jails, I attempted to develop a system to free these seriously disturbed inmates from solitary confinement and treat them in therapeutic communities. I had been impressed by recent successes using this treatment approach to empower addicted and mentally ill individuals to fight for their own recovery.

I found the physical conditions at the Tombs and several other city jails filthy, rat- and roach-infested, dark, cacophonous and, at best, anti-therapeutic. There is a distinctly powerful odor on prison cell blocks, more intense on those housing the mentally ill. It is a mixture of stale air, sweat, and excrement that survives all disinfectant and has persisted for the five decades since I first worked in a prison.

When I started, psychiatric evaluations and follow-ups were performed mainly through the bars of dimly lit cells. The only therapy was high doses of psychotropic drugs. Medication hoarding, sales, swapping, and overdoses were common. As the new prison mental-health team, we attempted to develop a more humane treatment program. As a result of our efforts, conditions improved and the suicide rate plummeted, at least for the first six months. However, I grew increasingly frustrated with the inability to establish a working agreement between mental health and custody, despite weekly meetings.

Today I understand how difficult it is to resolve this apparently inherent disagreement. I stayed at the helm of this health-delivery system for only about eighteen months and, once again, thought I'd never set foot in another prison.

Nevertheless, I became known as an expert in prison reform and mental-health care, and was subsequently asked to testify about many aspects of correctional treatment. Early cases included an inmate's right to choose to be housed in the "homosexual cell block" and denial of a correctional officer's right to be a member of the Ku Klux Klan. In the latter, I testified that even the thought of a white hood caused many inmates to become unduly anxious and paranoid. In this case, ACLU attorneys represented the corrections officers. I was struck by the moral dilemma of my being in an unaccustomed corner in the struggle for civil liberties.

In 1972, Texas prison inmate David Ruiz filed a complaint stating he faced unconstitutional conditions and was subjected to extreme circumstances in solitary confinement. His complaint, combined with others, became a class action suit (Ruiz v. Estelle) litigated by the U.S. attorney general on behalf of the inmates. The trial, which began in October 1978, lasted a year. I testified on the effects of overcrowding, sensory deprivation in solitary, and the lack of mental-health care. Judge William Justice, so ironically but aptly named, ruled that the conditions of imprisonment within this prison system were cruel and unusual punishment, and therefore unconstitutional. The decision led to federal oversight of the Texas Department of Criminal Justice, eventually changing how Texas prisons operated.

An early solution to overcrowding was to house inmates in single tents in the Texas wastelands, boiling hot in summer and freezing in winter. Conditions were supposedly resolved in 2001, and by early 2014 the state of Texas was being cited by experts as a model for prisons and sentencing reform, with a state crime rate at a fifty-year low.

For several years after I testified in Texas I felt changes brought about by my efforts were insignificant. However, it takes time to rebuild correctional systems.

When I read about Texas as a model of reform now, it would seem Judge Justice's rulings have finally made a difference thirty-five years after they were imposed. In 2004, the University of Texas, Austin, created the William Wayne Justice Center for Public Interest Law in his honor. This is certainly a response, at least in part, to his role in reforming the Texas prison system.

In 1978 I was appointed director of psychiatric services at UC Irvine Medical Center in Orange, California. For about a year I complied with a County of Orange contract that required the emergency psychiatric unit to accept every psychiatric patient brought to the facility for evaluation. In this time of dwindling resources, there were twice as many clients as beds, so patients were kept on gurneys in hallways, creating an unsafe and anti-therapeutic environment. I objected and announced we would not accept any patients after our limited beds were full.

A few months after we limited admissions, the county developed other facilities to deal with the overflow. However, I now realize my decision at least temporarily contributed to the ranks of the untreated, homeless mentally ill.

Today, police are handling even more mental-health crises in our streets and homes. They are making life-and-death diagnostic decisions for which they have little or no training. Mentally ill individuals are often beaten and accidentally killed in failed attempts to restrain them. According to a study by the Treatment Advocacy project, psychiatric patients are 16 times more likely to be killed by police than those not so afflicted. There are few public psychiatric facilities where these patients can be taken.

Psychiatric emergency rooms in LA and other big cities have many more patients than they can handle, with the numbers increasing rapidly. Rather than wait for a hospital bed to become available, police officers' only option is to take the mentally ill to jail. That also goes for addicts and alcoholics in life-threatening withdrawal as well as people with emotional problems that lead to suicide attempts and homelessness. Yes, any one of us can end up in a correctional setting that leaves us in a far worse state. On the other hand, frequent mistakes are made in evaluation, leaving untreated, psychotic mass murderers free to roam the streets and kill at will.

I moved from New York to California in 1977, interrupting my drive west to review mental-health care in the Utah correctional system. Conditions were little different here than they had been in Texas:

overcrowded, antiquated facilities with little or no ability to deal with the beginning influx of mentally ill inmates.

My first assignment at the University of California, Irvine, in 1977 was to supervise the school's elite psychiatry residents during a mandatory six-month rotation at Metropolitan State Hospital, Norwalk, California. There were thousands of severely disturbed patients at the facility then, spread over 162 acres in what I recall as ivy-covered red brick buildings interspersed with gnarled, aging trees.

Just as when I was at Rockland State, trainees there gravitated to the more therapeutic and unique programs at this state hospital. The trainees worked at a therapeutic community treating drug addicts and in a large ward that housed only patients who had become chronically psychotic after the ingestion of phencyclidine—PCP, or angel dust, as it was commonly called. Interestingly, after PCP abuse had become almost non-existent for over thirty years, it re-emerged in 2015 and has been slowly spreading coast to coast across the United States. In the past few years many new drugs that cause irreversible violent psychoses have arrived on the illicit drug scene, but public hospital units are not there to treat them. Instead, addicts end up in jails and prisons, even though they once led normal lives before taking stimulants, hallucinogens, and other designer drugs. These newer designer drugs also frequently produce a psychosis that may be irreversible even with proper treatment.

My experiences in this and other state systems gave me a broad perspective on the level of care provided as the medical institutions were eliminated. I was quite critical of the treatment, or lack of it, taking place in state hospitals, even though care had improved during this time, and populations of involuntary patients had already diminished considerably. In 1955 there were about 560,000 patients in state hospitals. By 2014 there were approximately 35,000. Where did they go? Not into well-developed community mental-health programs. They ended up homeless and incarcerated.

Current estimates of the mentally ill in jails and prisons rise as high as half a million. Of course, the overall population has doubled in these sixty years, leaving us with at least the statistical probability of a half million homeless mentally ill as well.

In 1987 I began an evaluation of Vacaville as part of a lawsuit filed by the US attorney general contesting the condition of mental health care at the facility. This was a medical/psychiatric facility within the California prison system, and the phasing out of state psychiatric hospitals had shifted over five hundred mentally disturbed inmates to the prison. About a third of these were as sick as any patients I had seen in psychiatric institutions throughout this country. I found a multitude of deficiencies at Vacaville, including a glaring lack of psychiatrists and other mental-health staff. Only six of twenty psychiatric positions were filled at the time I visited. Psychiatrists had left in a mass exodus because of low salaries, substandard working conditions, and responsibility without the means to implement curative measures.

The lack of mental-health providers led to an environment devoid of therapy, plus progressively greater difficulties recruiting new staff. Sixty percent of correctional officers were also polled as dissatisfied at this time, which reinforced the cycle of poor working conditions and paralyzed recruitment for all levels of staffing. Of course, correctional officers' problems are not limited to California. A study of guards in Michigan found that one-third had clinical depression and met criteria for post- traumatic stress disorder (PTSD).

The mentally ill were housed in solitary conditions at Vacaville, and what little therapy there was took place almost exclusively through the bars of locked cells.

Corrections had stopped using Tasers six months before my visit because this weapon had caused several deaths in patients on psychiatric medications. Several of the remedies suggested in this lawsuit, such as doubling salaries and creating more positions to meet mental-health needs, were eventually put into place. The prison hired new psychiatric staff, at least temporarily. But they, too, became disillusioned by conditions that made meaningful therapy almost impossible, and left Vacaville for better working conditions.

It is not surprising that many inmates committed suicide in this setting. The common urge to suicide in prisons was facilitated at Vacaville by inadequate monitoring and administration of medication, leading to widespread hoarding and overdoses.

Another problem in this facility was the impaired relationship between the California Department of Corrections and Rehabilitation (CDCR) and the maximum-security forensic hospital at Atascadero (ASH). This hospital had a capacity of 1,275 beds. Every patient at ASH was either court-committed or a transfer from a state correctional facility. Atascadero psychiatrists rejected 50 percent of referrals from CDCR, complaining their staff was burning out from the stress of dealing with patients from that system. This resulted in a backlog of extremely disturbed inmates in the state prisons, particularly at the prison psychiatric facility at Vacaville. The inability to refer out to ASH was a product not only of administrative red tape, but of how seriously ill and difficult these inmates were—and still are—for any system to handle. This problem was still quite present in my 2013-14 evaluation of CDCR.

Although my recommendations for more staff and higher salaries were eventually implemented, my plea for a more therapeutic environment was ignored, as was my warning that the accelerated closing down of state hospitals and lack of funds for community treatment would exacerbate the problem, and it did.

I continued my work in 1992 as an expert witness in the Coleman v. Wilson suit to reduce unconstitutional overcrowding in CDCR. The suit was brought against then Governor Pete Wilson and officials of the California Department of Corrections. I evaluated four California state prisons and reviewed medical records and data from several others. My findings did not substantially differ from those made five years earlier. Corrections still did not have adequate access to ASH. The inability to hire psychiatrists and other mental-health professionals was a continuing problem. Tehachapi State Prison, for example, had only one psychiatrist available every other weekend to handle the mental-health needs of over 5,500 inmates. There was a system wide inadequacy of medical records and little treatment beyond poorly administered medications.

An attempt was made to handle the lack of psychiatrists by hiring non-psychiatric physicians to prescribe psychiatric medications. This was almost as much of a problem as asking psychiatrists to do brain surgery. This practice was brought to a halt when the physicians staged a protest about the dangers of this practice.

Tasers, proved fatal to patients on psychotropic meds, and were totally gone by this time, replaced by potentially dangerous and anti-therapeutic 37-mm gas guns.

Medication hoarding, suicide by hanging, and overdosing continued to be rampant, as were the black market in medications and the importation of street drugs. Many, if not most, severely mentally ill inmates were housed in restrictive administrative segregation cells twenty-three hours a day, only a bit of stimulation short of total solitary confinement.

These conditions frequently led to psychosis and suicide. They were, and still are, antithetical to any sort of therapeutic approach.

Several of the suggestions I made in my 1993 report were implemented, including raising the salaries of psychiatrists and using a comprehensive mental-health team. However, the lack of a therapeutic environment and the attendant problems of dealing with difficult patients continued the progression of mental-health staff shortages.

I was not directly involved in the Coleman suits for constitutional care of the mentally ill as they subsequently evolved through several iterations of Coleman v. Wilson, (Gov. Gray) Davis, and (Gov. Arnold) Schwarzenegger. I continued some prison expert work over the next two decades, particularly involving the role of jail conditions and negligence in inmate suicides. I also testified to the harm the "rubber room" caused in dealing with acute mental disturbance. The rubber room is a sparse, rubber-lined cell that provides little opportunity for self-harm, but isolates the inmate with total lack of amenities and no direct supervision.

In 2013, I returned as an expert in Coleman v. (Gov. Jerry) Brown, in part because I could compare my knowledge of the system as it had been twenty years ago to the present. I felt my additional years of experience gave me a greater perspective on the merits of the positions of corrections officials as well as that of the inmates. The United States and many other countries had changed their attitude toward criminal justice in those two decades. Jails and prisons everywhere were overflowing with drug-addicted and seriously mentally ill prisoners.

I am not against the continued existence of prisons in our society, but I am vehemently opposed to attempting to treat the vast numbers of the mentally ill in inappropriate and punitive correctional settings. I have often been asked under cross- examination, "Doctor, isn't it true that you believe a mentally ill person should never be in prison?" The question always brings me to an inner sigh and a long pause. I suppose there are some violent inmates and psychotic murderers who are so resistant to treatment they could never be handled in any setting outside of a jail or prison; but even then, treatment should be in a humane and calming environment.

I am also aware of society's need for prisons as a deterrent, to provide temporary safety to the community, and even for retribution. However, we need institutions that also rehabilitate, and do not lead to recidivism and progression of criminal activity. They must be tied into adequate systems of community services, including housing, appropriate jobs, and treatment as will be described in subsequent chapters.

The stories revealed during my most recent observations are the subjects of many of the chapters that follow.

I have chosen to tell these tales in narrative form rather than in academic style. The names of inmates and other identifying data have been changed to preserve their anonymity, but the facts of individual experience and prison environment are depicted as accurately as I can recall or obtain from record reviews and interviews. Reproduced court testimony is public record, but is edited to avoid grammatical errors and the tediousness of literal testimony.

CHAPTER 2

Early Experiences as a Prison Psychiatrist

LEWISBURG FEDERAL PENITENTIARY WAS DESIGNED in a French Renaissance architectural style with a few gothic arches thrown in. Located in the midst of rolling farmland, the prison was separated from the bucolic countryside by brick walls, metal, and barbed wire fences. Nearby Bucknell University offered faculty volunteers for the prison and a network of friends for my wife and me. We found a spacious farmhouse to rent, and the owner, a local gun manufacturer, remodeled it according to our needs and taste. The oldest covered bridge in Pennsylvania was at the edge of our property, spanning a rushing stream in the spring. Our lovely home and contacts with nearby Bucknell, which included my appointment as part-time psychiatrist, helped make our exodus from New York City tolerable during our first experience outside of a big city.

Many infamous inmates have been incarcerated at the Lewisburg penitentiary, including gangster Al Capone, union leader Jimmy Hoffa, civil rights activist Bayard Rustin, psychologist Wilhelm Reich, and accused spy Alger Hiss. Harry Gold, a convicted spy whose testimony resulted in the trial and execution of Julius and Ethel Rosenberg, directed the prison lab while I was working there. Tino De Angelis, the subject of Norman C. Miller's Pulitzer Prize-winning book, *The Great Salad Oil Swindle*, came to Lewisburg for a psychiatric evaluation during my tenure. Their stays at Lewisburg are public record so I have chosen to name them directly.

I was assigned two inmate clerks, Jess and Rob. Both of them were from New York City and there on drug-related charges. Working for the psychiatrist was a coveted job at the prison. For some reason it was almost as desirable as working for the chaplain. I was never sure why, but it certainly was better than washing dishes or cleaning toilets. I relied on my two aides to tell me what was going on beneath the obvious, and which guards I could trust to train and work with mentally ill inmates.

Jess was a short, curly-haired Jewish man in his forties from Brooklyn. I had as much communication with him as with anyone at the prison. He got into trouble only once when he refused to tell authorities which of his fellow inmates had committed a minor offense.

Jess told me what really happened, but I pledged not to tell anyone. I did not participate in his hearing because of a conflict of interest. He was sent to the Hole, but for only a brief stay. Jess and Rob both communicated with me soon after they were released from prison. Jess became a drug counselor at a methadone clinic, and he and his wife came to our Manhattan brownstone with a motorized model plane for my recently born son. Rob was quickly incarcerated in the Tombs and asked for help defending himself against a new offense.

The institutional psychologist was in the office next to mine. He had survived the tenure of many psychiatrists before me. When I met him, he was already co-opted and burnt out. He advised me to follow in his footsteps and not make waves in the system.

Just upstairs from my office was a nine-bed psychiatric unit where we housed mentally ill inmates and some individuals found guilty of federal crimes but who required psychiatric evaluation prior to sentencing.

The patients on this unit were seen daily by a medical-technical assistant (MTA) and me, and the unit was staffed 24/7 by inmate trustees. Most of the

MTAs were retired Army medics, and more identified with corrections than with treatment. The housing consisted of single cells, but the doors were open all day to a small day room. I recall only a few minor problems on this psychiatric ward, all of which were easily handled. My major dilemma was figuring out who needed psychiatric care and who was manipulating to be housed on the unit for some sort of secondary gain. Of course, some inmates wanted to be on this unit because they knew it was a place where they could get fair and humane treatment.

Lewisburg had a special program to handle mentally ill inmates who were outside of the psychiatric unit, which permitted them to work as part of a particular unit, accompanied by an understanding corrections officer. This group was euphemistically called "the coal pile," a name given to this job detail in the past when inmates did indeed shovel coal. The officer in charge was part of a group of guards I trained in understanding human behavior and basic techniques of group counseling. He was firm but understanding. The ability to work was therapeutic for this group of mentally disturbed inmates and so much better than keeping them in solitary confinement as is so commonly done.

The inmates tested me in many ways at first. They tried to get meds from me to get high or at least relieve the pain of imprisonment. I didn't observe evidence of drug smuggling at Lewisburg as I did at every other prison I later evaluated. I did have to render emergency medical care to one prisoner because he had a fever of 104 degrees. He confided to me that he had fermented a pulp of ragweed and injected it intravenously, quite a step beyond the traditional prison wine or Pruno, made from fermented fruit and catsup. Another inmate appeared to ask innocently for chewing gum. I brought him a pack of Wrigley's before I learned it was contraband. Gum could make impressions of locks that then could be used to make keys.

Many of my psychiatric contacts at Lewisburg were memorable. One inmate I saw in weekly individual psychotherapy I will call Sweets O'Rourke. He was called Sweets because he could smooth talk anyone, particularly a woman, to get whatever he wanted. His brooding, dark handsomeness certainly worked with the women he wished to conquer. But I too was conned—if indeed it was a con—by the tale he wove of his bank robberies. He had been previously diagnosed as bipolar, or manic-depressive, as it was then termed. He explained that he only robbed banks when he was in a manic phase.

The robberies gave him more driven energy and euphoria, which he then used to charm and have sex with as many conquests as he possibly could.

In our therapy together I had the same understanding with him that I had with all inmates. I would not prepare any report that would enhance or hamper his parole. I hoped this stipulation would help him be totally honest with me rather than use treatment as a means to help him get an early release. In therapy, he described his father as brutal and distant.

However, his dad had a coin collection. When he and his father sat together and his father taught him about the coins, he felt a closeness and warmth. Sweets had been his mother's favorite among his large group of siblings, alienating him still further from his father.

Sweets shared in therapy that after he robbed a bank he loved to fondle the wrappers that held rolls of coins. He denied he received pleasure from fondling the actual coins or bills he had stolen. But caressing the wrappers was a great aphrodisiac for him, driving him to more and more sexual encounters. Fresh from a psychoanalytically oriented training program, I interpreted his bank robberies and coin wrapper fetish as an attempt to get close to his distant father. Then, by incorporating his father's power, he was able to feel potent with women. He had a mild "aha" moment with this insight, which we worked through with his dreams, fantasies, and transference to me as an accepting paternal presence.

O'Rourke finished his sentence shortly after I left the prison, and I didn't hear from him for several years.

Evidently our "Freudian" therapy was not too successful. I received a call from his attorney in Washington, DC, informing me Sweets had robbed a bank and wanted me to testify to the role of mental illness in his crime. I reevaluated him in a federal holding facility, and in the interview he was in a full-blown manic state.

He greeted me with a warm but cunning Jack Nicholson smile. As he revealed the details of his crime, he became so enthralled that his mania intensified; he spoke faster and faster as he progressed to full euphoria. His energy was so infectious, I too felt a bit high—as I often do with euphoric, manic individuals. After the robbery, he told me, he quickly got on an airplane to get away. Once the plane took off, he rubbed his hands over the coin wrappers. He said he became so excited he quickly seduced a flight attendant and renewed his membership in the mile-high club. He then spent the night with her and his coin wrappers in a hotel room as soon as they landed.

The next time I saw Sweets was in a federal courtroom where he was on trial for bank robbery. In my testimony, I emphasized his manic state at the time of the robbery as a manifestation of psychosis. The prosecuting attorney attacked this with the then-existing version of the insanity defense, which found guilt when there was the ability to commit a criminal act with planned, rational action regardless of the presence of mental illness.

However, this attorney really went after my interpretation of the psychodynamics of the case. He attempted to discredit my entire testimony on the basis of his exaggerated reframe of my psychological formulation. I can still hear his booming, challenging voice when he scowled and asked me, "Now, Doctor, you mean to say he stole the money so he could stroke the coin wrappers and get an erection and seduce a stewardess?"

Needless to say, Sweets was sentenced to return to federal prison, undoubtedly this time without psychoanalytic psychotherapy.

I took part in the struggle to make the conditions in solitary confinement at Lewisburg more humane, even though I had strong feelings it should never be used. During my tenure, inmates in solitary were, for the first time, given: mattresses for eight hours at night, their own eyeglasses, dentures, and a toothbrush. Later on, several nationwide lawsuits against the damaging effects of solitary resulted mainly in changing the name to secure housing unit or SHU and possibly, but rarely, one hour daily out of the cell. To inmates it was still the Hole. There was a bit more light in most cells, but the SHU still led to all the damaging effects of sensory deprivation including anxiety, depression, suicide, and psychoses. Administrative segregation was only slightly less restrictive and quite close to the conditions of solitary confinement. As will be discussed later, a critical part of the 2014 Coleman lawsuit was a challenge to housing the mentally ill in any form of solitary except temporarily, under the most urgent of circumstances.

I conducted group therapy with the custodial officers themselves as part of their training, as well as to offer them the opportunity to vent about their personal trauma as a result of working in this setting. This gave me my first opportunity to empathize with the problems of corrections workers. They shared with me their fears that if solitary and other punitive practices were banned, they would have no means to control the prisoners; they feared anarchy and chaos would result.

This was a warning to me about the officers' own paranoia and what can happen when changes in this type of system are made too quickly. On the other hand, the system tends to right itself and resist rapid change. My later experiences in the California prisons taught me that it requires decades of constant legal, political, and journalistic pressure for meaningful shifts to occur and continue.

A number of diverse political forces came together in 1971 to create an unusual opportunity for me to help change the New York City prison system. John Lindsay had been mayor for four years and wanted to humanize the city jails. Pressure was on him to make changes because of a high suicide rate.

His office stood behind me in my only prerequisite for taking the job: all mental health staff had to be removed from the corrections budget and placed under the director of psychiatry of the City Health Services Administration. This move gave me an illusion of autonomy, which was quickly threatened when I learned of a preexisting regulation stating that no matter whom my staff reported to, the warden was ultimately in charge of every program (and every person) at the institution.

Weekly meetings were held between corrections and mental health for over a year. A memorandum of understanding was drafted, and not one point in the memo was ever agreed upon. After over fifty years of experience with prisons, I now recognize the inherent difficulty in reconciling the disagreement between the goals and practices of corrections and treatment. These differences have been present in every penal institution I have ever walked into. I have yet to see them resolved satisfactorily. I wonder how this will settle out in Cook County now that a psychologist has been appointed warden.

Another factor that intrigued me in my position in New York was new federal funding to provide a unique type of employee in this system. These programs provided salaries for 44 positions, immediately doubling the mental health staff. These individuals were all paraprofessionals. They had to be either recovering addicts with at least one year of sobriety, or ex-inmates who had graduated from a prison rehabilitation program and demonstrated at least one year of contributing to society in a meaningful way. These workers were almost all minorities from NYC ghettos. Funding was also available for several experienced supervisors and a supportive group-processing program for the new staff. Here I was, helping to make major changes take place even as the long-term institutional psychologists again warned me not to make waves.

A career ladder was created. It granted an associate of arts degree after three years of part-time schooling and on-the-job training for indigenous workers, who had themselves been scarred by the slums and managed to survive. There was also funding for sixty new mental-health workers of all disciplines. I hired every minority professional I could find for these positions, yet the Urban League stormed into my office and challenged me about why I had hired so many para-professionals and so few minority professionals. This was my initiation into the well-known caveat that it is impossible to please all factions when it comes to politics. Perhaps that is what politicians can appear to do best.

I was by this time familiar with the utilization of paraprofessionals. I had worked with a program staffed only by recovering addicts at Reality House, an outpatient drug treatment program in the center of Harlem. I was inspired by their energy, commitment, and achievements, and had published several aca-demic articles analyzing their therapeutic techniques and successes. This type of treatment was emerging in many other venues with clients who were relatively untreatable using traditional psychiatric techniques. It was conceptually "the use of the product of a problem to treat a problem" and was adapted from the Synanon drug rehabilitation program by many other programs, including Daytop Village and Phoenix House. These programs started in New York and rapidly spread across the country, establishing therapeutic commu-nities in neighborhoods, jails, and prisons.

Recovering paraprofessionals have a great under-standing of the inmates' culture and difficulties at the same time as they are attuned to their manipulations. On the other hand, they have more difficulty working within not one, but two, bureaucratic agencies than those of us who have been raised to deal with authoritarian structures. Each of the two powerful bureaucracies were much more difficult to deal with than any single one I had previously—and perhaps subsequently—experienced in my own career.

To make matters far worse, the New York City system was undergoing budget freezes that conflicted with the federal funding even as we were trying to add staff. As a result, we were unable to bring aboard many people we had committed to, and we had to pay the newly hired for the delay. These problems would frustrate anyone, particularly my "recovering" staff, who were waiting for jobs and pay while living below poverty level.

I was too inexperienced at the time to appreciate the stress on corrections of introducing a hundred new staff to the system so quickly, particularly since so many had been homeless or done jail time. I was shocked when I learned that one of the very talented psychologists I had hired was a member of the Black Panthers, and corrections had banned her from working inside the prisons. I trusted and respected her abilities, and placed her in charge of the aftercare program we had just established. I felt honored by her presence when she attended a presentation I gave at a psychoanalytic meeting on the psychology of prisons in society.

We attempted to develop a comprehensive program throughout the ten institutions that comprised the NYC jail system. We began with enhanced screening. To screen new admissions to these jails we utilized a paraprofessional to screen new admissions with the supervision of a psychologist. Wherever possible, the relevant probation officer was contacted to establish alternatives to incarceration as one aspect of a treatment plan.

The treatment team would attempt to implement the best course during incarceration and plan for aftercare when early diversion was not possible. Since this system evaluated over 100,000 admissions yearly, screening was available to only a fraction of inmates, but it served as a model. We were also able to train some corrections officers and physicians to conduct a more thorough initial assessment than they had in the past.

Prior to my arrival all mental observation (MO) patients were housed one or two persons to a five-by-eight-by-eight-foot cell. Those who were seriously disturbed were kept in their cells constantly, and those who were less so were permitted in a limited recreation area with few facilities. Fortunately, a fifty-five-bed dormitory on Rikers Island was remodeled just prior to my arrival, and awaiting staffing and programming. We were also able to develop several smaller units at other jails and free up 25 psychiatric beds at Bellevue Hospital.

Within six months of operation, 100 mentally disturbed inmates were treated in settings meeting or surpassing traditional psychiatric standards. Adequate treatment in prisons raised another citywide controversy. Why should prisoners receive better care than the mentally ill do in community hospitals? I continue to see letters to the editor carry this message whenever reform of prison mental health or prison conditions in general becomes an issue. The obvious answer is that both systems need to be fixed.

We implemented four basic treatment principles in the ten NYC jails. First, we brought in a full complement of psychiatric treatment modalities. These included occupational, recreational, and music therapy; proper medication; and individual and group psychotherapy. The second basic approach was the use of paraprofessionals who had been able to extricate themselves from the same ghettos as the inmates.

The third was to establish therapeutic communities where inmates assumed responsibility for themselves and other fellow mental patients. This was successful in preventing suicides but less so in developing individual autonomy because it placed inmates in conflict with the values of the prison society. Prison values are authoritarian and stifle the individual's ability to make his or her own decisions. The fourth was to use a continuum of care and other components of community mental health.

The major problem with establishing therapeutic environments was our relationship with custody and our inability to develop a working agreement with the department. The officers assigned to these units could not be specially selected, according to corrections policy. Even officers whom corrections termed *instant riot* were permitted to work in these special programs. Inmates didn't trust these officers, believing they would use the information shared in therapy against them. On the other hand, officers whom we considered therapeutic were not permitted to participate in group therapy or treatment planning.

At first the patients themselves made treatment difficult by making blackjacks out of occupational materials, or committing acts of violence or rape in the dormitories. Ultimately inmates on these units calmed down, treatment staff learned to set limits, and these destructive activities became less frequent on treatment units than in the general population.

Another component was to have a treatment team consisting of a psychiatrist, social worker, psychologist, and several paraprofessionals at each of the ten NYC jails. Our goal was to provide screening, social services, proper medication, and individual and group psychotherapy to disturbed inmates in general population. Impediments included inadequate space to perform these therapies and security regulations. Inmates were only made available to come to clinics four hours daily, and even during these hours appointments were often canceled because of a shortage of escort officers. Officers assigned to this task were the first to be moved to other posts.

Another essential aspect of the program was consultation with correctional authorities. Despite our difficulties in establishing a mutual letter of agreement, there were many ways we did work together. A psychologist screened all corrections officer applicants, and a psychiatrist evaluated all officers considered for promotion. Many of the newer officers were themselves minorities from urban ghettos. They entered the system with enthusiasm but quickly became cynical and embittered after being exposed to inadequate, aging, and overcrowded facilities; angry inmates; and burnt-out long-term officers. When asked to identify with an inmate's despair, they preferred to complain about their own hopelessness. They were forced to work overtime and waited a year to receive the extra pay. Their daily absentee rate was the highest of any city uniformed service and was over 20 percent at some prisons.

My observations foreshadowed the results of the well-known prison experiment conducted by Stanford psychologist Phillip Zimbardo. This 1971 study randomly divided college students into inmates and guards. The study continues to be cited and discussed whenever the brutality of corrections officers is discussed. The issues raised by this investigation continue to be so topical that a film, *The Stanford Prison Experiment*, was released in the summer of 2015.

The subjects who played the role of guards became so sadistic—and the inmates so depressed and hopeless—that the research had to be terminated after only six days of a planned two weeks.

Retraining of prison guards had been absent for years in New York City.

Fortunately, during my tenure the Urban League gave corrections one week of sensitivity training every two years. I doubted this would reverse guards' co-option by the system, but at least it was a start.

As a result of media and political pressure, the city corrections commissioner began to add a few humane and therapeutic practices to the lives of inmates. These included weekend furloughs, more flexible visitation, marriage ceremonies, inmate suicide watches, and even inmate-staff councils.

We developed an aftercare program led by the previously mentioned Black Panther psychologist to provide treatment continuity and reverse the cycle of recidivism. Staff from this program met with institutional mental-health workers and the inmates one month before release to plan a comprehensive program including family counseling, housing, vocational training, education, and mental-health treatment. The New York Department of Vocational Rehabilitation provided a full-time specialist for this project. Paraprofessionals met inmates upon release and escorted them to their new program. Aftercare placed two-thirds of referrals into residential treatment or jobs.

An arrangement was made with a community religious group to place together eight carefully selected individuals awaiting trial for felonies in a communal apartment and help them obtain jobs prior to trial. With jobs in hand and a place to live, they had a better chance to be placed on probation instead of being incarcerated.

Unfortunately, the aftercare program could only reach 600 inmates yearly, a mere fraction of the 100,000 who went through the system. However, it served as a pilot project, proving recidivism could be reversed. Successful programs that are limited in time and reach only a fraction of offenders are common in corrections.

Obviously, a system of aftercare that interfaces with other social service programs is essential for any jail program to succeed. Our objectives involved working with agencies that were amenable to a co-operative effort, such as state hospitals, court clinics, judges, parole officers, clergy, the Legal Aid Society, universities, and vocational training programs.

Clearly I could not alter the societal problems at the core of our overcrowded jails, like housing, welfare, racism, mental-health services, employment, availability of street drugs, and education. These social issues lead to never-ending cycles of poverty, addiction, unemployment, recurrent criminal behavior, incarceration, and probation violations.

To resolve the multiple problems with jails and prisons, we need community reform before, during, and after incarceration. In an article I wrote about these issues in 1973, I stated: "As state hospitals reduce their census and become more and more 'open,' their ability to hold the potentially dangerous mentally disturbed inmate becomes progressively less." At that time I could not have dreamed how devastating the problem would be forty years later.

However, many experts clearly believe that improving prison conditions diverts attention from these underlying issues and that societal problems should be our major focus for change.

I hoped we had created an opening into more effective treatment of prisoners in NYC jails. Recent news stories suggest guard brutality continues to be a serious issue there. Mary Buser spent five years in the mental-health department at Rikers, NYC's largest prison facility, working her way up to assistant chief of the mental-health unit there by the time she left in 2005. In her book, *Lockdown On Rikers*, she describes constant beatings of inmates by guards despite then-Mayor Giuliani's "mission of violence reduction." An op-ed article written by Cecily McMillan and published in the July 23, 2014, issue of *The New York Times* leads me to believe that guard brutality is still a problem at Rikers. She said the city was investigating more than 100 violent assaults by guards on inmates. Nearly 80 percent of those who were beaten were suffering from mental illness. A few days later, the U.S. attorney in Manhattan reported there was a "deep-seated culture of violence" on the part of Rikers corrections officers.

On August 5, 2014, a *New York Times* editorial called for the city "to completely reform the culture of the jail system to ensure that violence is no longer tolerated." A May 2015 lawsuit filed by two women who had been incarcerated on Rikers alleged they were sexually abused or raped by eight corrections officers. The suit further states that rape is "endemic" there and that the City of New York has been unwilling to address the issue. Efforts to reform guards' behavior were met with stiff resistance from Norman Seabrook, the head of the correction officers' union, whom *The New York Times* called "the biggest obstacle to curb brutality" at Rikers Island.

The Correctional Association of New York has been monitoring prison conditions for over a hundred years. It described rampant beatings of inmates by prison guards and concluded in 2015 "the ghosts of Attica will continue to wail until prison guards are no longer allowed to beat and brutalize people with relative impunity."

In a May 2, 2015, op-ed column in *The New York Times*, Ross Douthat described how strongly the corrections officers' union can bias public policy toward its own interests: "In California over the last few decades, the correctional officers' union first lobbied for a prison-building spree and then well-entrenched, exercised veto power over criminal justice reform." This union contributed almost two million dollars to Gov. Jerry Brown's gubernatorial campaign in 2011. I wonder if this helps explain the otherwise liberal governor's stance in defending the status quo in California's beleaguered prison system.

In July 2015, *The New York Times* documented 99 cases over two years in which mentally ill Rikers inmates were beaten so severely they needed emergency medical care. Kalief Browder, a 16-year-old African-American, began a stay of over a thousand days at Rikers in 2010, mostly in solitary confinement. When not in solitary he was assaulted by a guard, and pummeled and kicked by a large group of inmates, which was confirmed by video surveillance. He attempted suicide several times while in jail and killed himself after his release from prison. He attributed his then-significant mental illness and desperation to the time he spent in solitary. Browder's story and video were made public by *The New Yorker* magazine, bringing NYC Mayor Bill de Blasio's attention to the brutality at Rikers.

In November 2014, de Blasio called Rikers Island a dehumanizing environment and allocated $32.5 million to establish new units for the mentally ill, transgender, and most violent inmates. He also mandated a great reduction in the use of punitive segregation and increased the use of security cameras.

Despite his efforts, 500 people attended the Facebook event "March to Shut Down Rikers – Justice for Kalief Browder! No to Criminalization!" on June 27, 2015. Despite the protestors' peaceful demands for mental-health services, correction officers with attack dogs met them as they approached the institution.

A 2015 law passed in New York State required that any inmate treated for mental illness would get continued mental-health treatment facilitated by enrollment in Medicaid and initial clinic appointments as part of discharge planning.

I hope these actions and other recent developments reflect a national movement toward prison reform and attention to the problems of the mentally ill, despite the continued brutality described above in California and New York. I hope it does not reflect another cycle where a local liberal leader attempts to make changes, which are then reversed by more conservative replacements.

On June 17, 2015, an L.A. County Jail sheriff's deputy told a federal jury he and three other officers beat a handcuffed man in a jail visitor's center, claiming the man had attacked them. Two officers were found guilty of using excessive force and falsifying records, apparently common practices in corrections facilities. One officer was sentenced to six years in federal prison and the other received a sentence of seven years.

In July 2015, the *LA Times* reported an inmate was shackled without food for 32 hours, and ten LA county jail employees were relieved of duty as a result.

These two cases are just the tip of the iceberg when it comes to this type of violent guard behavior at LA County jails, but they are also evidence that these problems are now being exposed, and officials are beginning to deal with them.

The local jail in my own Southern California County of Orange is not immune to prison guard violence. In March 2015, a patient of mine endured a three-day stay at the Orange County Men's Jail following a drug-induced psychosis. He described the brutality he observed during his brief stay. "The guards picked out the biggest, toughest looking man in the holding cell. Four of them grabbed him, threw him on the ground and beat him to a pulp. The sergeant turned to us and said they would do the same to any motherfucker who did not obey them."

Similar violent incidents are duplicated every day at jails and prisons nationwide, often aimed at the mentally ill. Most, however, are more reactive and not such pure examples of show of force as the incident above.

Present Problems with Criminalization

CHAPTER 3

The Prison Gladiator

I WATCHED ANOTHER POWERFUL VIDEO of the forcible cell extraction of a mentally ill inmate during my February 2013 assessment of use of force in California prisons. Much of the apparent inhumane brutality described in my prologue of a cell extraction was repeated in this incident. I later learned, however, that many of the underlying issues were quite different in the case of this inmate, whom I will name Sidney. He was transferred to another facility just before I came to see the tapes, and I must admit I was somewhat suspicious—perhaps even paranoid—about why he was not there for my scheduled interview.

At the time of his forcible extraction, Sidney was been housed in a mental health crisis bed in a hospital unit at Corcoran State Prison. This is the highest level of prison mental-health care. He was so psychotic he was hallucinating, paranoid and smearing shit all over himself.

His skin hung loosely over his large frame. His beard was scruffy, his Afro wild and amorphous His eyes were filled with fear but blank and peering right through me as I watched the tape. A psychiatrist, whom he disliked and mistrusted, ordered involuntary intramuscular medication, which Sidney refused. A "controlled" use of force for a cell extraction began twenty-five minutes later. As mentioned in the prologue, controlled use of force is less commonly used and not as brutal as spontaneous use of force, which is never recorded.

The process began with a psychologist mumbling what was called a "clinical intervention" through a heavy cell door in a feeble attempt to get Sidney to agree voluntarily to be medicated. A group of eight or nine custody officers introduced themselves on the video, most suited up from head to toe in protective gear and gas masks. They repeatedly ordered Sid, an obviously psychotic inmate-patient, to "cuff up" or "submit to handcuffs." They shouted these phrases over and over without any other attempt at communication. Although Sidney couldn't understand or comply with these orders, each of his failures to cuff up was met by another massive injection of toxic pepper spray (oleoresin capsicum or OC) into the cell. He repeatedly cried, "Help me, somebody please help me!" But there was no attempt by officers or clinicians to understand what was really going on or to offer any help. His pleas were met only by more and more toxic OC spray. As Sid's fear escalated, the guards became more and more gruff and menacing.

The female captain who ordered the cell extraction stated in her incident report that Sidney was "observed in a mental state where he could not follow the simplest instruction. When ordered to submit to handcuffs he responded, 'How do I do that?' although staff repeatedly explained to him he needed to back up to the cuff port and place his hands through the opening. He was still very confused and disoriented with complying with instructions."

Yet even after the captain observed his confusion and lack of understanding about what was going on, she permitted a sergeant to disperse one continuous burst of pepper spray from an MK-09 approximately four feet from the inmate. These large canisters and bursts of OC are generally used to control crowds of protestors and are considered by experts to be dangerous in small, closed-in areas.

Sidney continued to refuse to be handcuffed until the officers finally grabbed one hand and attached it to a heavy metal triangle through the food port. He repeatedly pulled the other hand back each time the guard's hand came near his and asked, "What's going on?" When there was no answer, he plaintively whined, "I want to go home." When the officers finally decided to open the door of the cell and physically remove Sidney, he appeared poised to exit voluntarily. Nevertheless, the officers rushed him with a full-length shield, shoving him back into a cell filled with OC spray. He repeatedly cried out in anguish for help: "Why is this happening to me?" and "Why isn't anybody listening to me?"

As I watched the tape, I found myself saying aloud, "C'mon guys. Please listen to him. You are torturing him. He doesn't know what you are asking him to do. He's becoming more and more paranoid. Can't you see this?"

The officers dragged him from the cell and behind the open door, but the camera was not repositioned. Consequently, all I could see on the video was a morass of officers bearing down upon his naked limbs. I couldn't see if the officers were pummeling him or attempting to restrain him against his fear-driven resistance. His screams at that point were like those of an anguished, badly wounded animal. I could only make out, "Oh no! Help!" amid the wailing. In the skirmish he suffered several cuts on his fingers and an injury to his wrist so severe it required long-term medical attention.

He was placed on a gurney with each of his limbs and his waist immobilized with heavy leather straps. Like John in the prologue, he was filmed nude, with his genitals flaring. Once he was unable to move his trunk and limbs except to squirm in place, multiple custody officers held him down for forced injections of a powerful anti-psychotic medication. He was still able to swing his head back and forth wildly, requiring two more officers to press his head down.

He became even more frightened and pleaded, "I didn't do nothing wrong . . . I don't want to decapitate nobody . . . my head hurts . . . I don't want to kill people . . . I don't want this to happen to me . . . I don't want to be executed." He was not decontaminated after the extraction, although prison policy mandates this to prevent the toxic OC spray from continuing to irritate the inmate's skin. He was then transferred to a barren seclusion and restraint room where he was strapped down onto a specially made bed with five thick, wide leather belts attached.

As a result of this incident, Sidney was charged with a rule violation for what Corrections terms "obstructing a peace officer in the performance of his duties in the use of force." The prison task force assigned to review the incident concluded only that all current policies were followed. Its only criticism was that Sidney's genitalia were exposed on the video.

The clinician who completed the mental health assessment stated, "Inmate's mental-health state included delusions/false thoughts/paranoia and didn't seem to understand consequences of not complying with a custody officer." His recommendation: "Inmate will benefit from therapy and activities that provide reality orientation . . . social interaction/talking with others, and things that help prompt his memory."

Nevertheless, Sid was found guilty of "obstruction," and his prison stay was extended 90 days through loss of earned "good time," just like every one of dozens of other extractions I reviewed. He also lost 30 days of all privileges that would provide any human contact, to be put into effect after his release from the mental-health crisis bed. Consequently, even when released from the prison hospital, he would be deprived of virtually all of his opportunities for external stimuli, which would further isolate him, increase his paranoia and anxiety, and contribute to his needing to return to a mental-health bed.

When Sidney was finally released from a treatment unit he was housed in segregation under conditions of isolation and lack of social contact, where he again decompensated and cycled back and forth for months after the extraction. These punishments totally contradict every recommendation made by the mental health clinician. It is no wonder there are massive mental-health staff shortages, sick days and burnout. Their therapeutic recommendations are simply ignored.

Sidney was finally released to his hometown, and his attorney offered me the opportunity to interview him in person about a year after I first saw the tape. I was enthused about speaking with him and understanding his version of the mental-health treatment he received while in prison.

I met with Sid at his aunt's law office in a well-appointed building in Ventura County. The lobby was elegantly designed with a salt-water fish tank and travertine fountain. How different this was from my interviews of the other patients I had seen on the tapes. These had taken place with the inmates in wrist and foot shackles in the cages corrections called therapeutic modules.

During a short wait by the fountain I learned the aunt's son was a recent murder victim and I was in the midst of a family in mourning. The deceased was Sid's cousin, and like a brother to him. He had been shot in the chest and killed in a gang drive-by a few days before. Grieving relatives told me he wasn't in the gang, just hanging out. I wondered why I was meeting Sidney in the midst of such family grief.

However, he was eager to speak with me, so I began the interview in his aunt's tastefully furnished office.

What a difference between the man before me and the one on the tape. I couldn't even come close to recognizing him. He was clean-shaven, and his soft brown skin glistened. His head had been shaved a few days before, and he was well dressed in a black T-shirt and neatly pressed jeans. He was six-feet-five inches tall and had gained about fifty pounds. He politely sneezed into his forearm on several occasions. He reminded me of a gentle Geoffrey Holder playing Punjab in the film *Annie*, but I could sense a boiling cauldron of anger just beneath his soft, halting voice.

The first thing Sidney wanted me to know in my personal interview was, "A week after I was maced, a guard came up to me and said, 'Congratulations, that was the toughest scuffle I've ever had.' He wanted to shake my hand, but I wouldn't touch him because I had to hold back from hitting him." This officer sounded to me like he experienced the brutal extraction as a sporting battle between equally empowered gladiators, while Sidney experienced it as a gang of slaveholders relentlessly beating and raping him.

As the interview progressed, Sidney expressed several delusional fears that helped me understand why this cell extraction was one of the worst experiences of his life. "I heard another inmate say, 'Take it like a man.' What that meant to me was they were going to rape me. That was the worst part."

It is not a rare occurrence that inmates urge each other to take as many hits of pepper spray as they can. In this context, 'take it like a man' has nothing to do with homosexuality. It is an urging more related to taking as many whiplashes as one can without crying, so the master knows he cannot defeat you. Once again we see the gladiator more as the beaten slave.

"When I saw the stretcher nearby and the way that guy snatched my arm, I thought they would put an implant in my body, make me a cyborg. My voices told me what was going to happen to me like they were premonitions. Why would anyone need a stretcher if they weren't planning to hurt me?"

His entire body trembled when he said, "I thought they'd come in with a chain saw and cut off my limbs. I feared they'd chop me up. They'd put a fake heart in me. I didn't want to be decapitated. They covered my eyes with a spit mask, which made me feel they'd cut me up. That was the worst day of my life."

I asked Sid if the extraction continued to affect him now.

His face dropped, and his body slumped. "I don't feel like the same person, as a man, as a living creature. I spent the next three days in five-point restraints. [In five-point restraints, an individual's hands, feet, legs and chest are tightly strapped to a bed designed for that purpose. It is unusual for a patient to be so subdued for more than a few hours.] I was unable to move. The experience made me feel even worse. I felt so docile afterwards. It broke my strength. I don't feel the same mental strength. I don't feel like I am the person I had built myself up to be."

Sid looked down and paused before he continued. "That broke me. I'm not close to the same person. I felt my whole being stripped. I am so far now from what I was."

"What made this cell extraction worse than any of the others you'd had in the past?" I asked Sidney.

"The severity of what I thought would happen to me," he promptly replied. "I heard them say, 'Where do we go? We'll go with the plan.' I thought they were taking me to the surgery room because I could see that part of the hospital. There was a guy in plain-clothes. I thought he was there to buy my parts. Every action they did was 100 percent proof of what they were going to do to me."

Everything that Sid experienced and saw was incorporated into his escalating fears and paranoid delusional system. After he was given injections of antipsychotic meds while placed in restraints, his fears continued but gradually became more rational.

I asked, "What about the five points? Why were they so difficult for you this time?"

"The dude who held my head down put his hand on my throat. They wouldn't let me use the bathroom, and I couldn't use the urinal lying on my back. They kept putting the spit mask on my face. I had a little rash. I kept trying to get up to get someone to talk to. The hardest part was they kept me in five points for three days. I didn't know why."

Another cause of Sidney's paranoia was his lack of trust in his Corcoran State Prison psychiatrist, Dr. X, who became an object of paranoia as well as part of the problem.

Sidney described his experience of Dr. X. "He stood over me when I was in restraints, leaned closer. It felt like he was the dude who said to me, 'Take it like a man.' I didn't like any of my experiences with X. He kept ridiculing me, mocking me. Once when we had met in the past, I was looking down to avoid eye contact and he said, 'You're looking at your penis and thinking of me.' "

I asked, "What do you still feel about the extraction?"

"I relive it like it's happening again," Sidney replied. "It drifts in and out of my mind like a dream while I watch TV."

"Do you ever dream about these events?"

"I wake up from a dream, and before I fully awaken, the extraction flashes through my head. That day, I feel weaker all day."

He continued to have paranoid symptoms even as we spoke, but with some insight. "I'm so paranoid. I think Corcoran [State Prison] has ties to my community now. Sometimes I even think my mom is part of the conspiracy. I fear that whatever plot the people at Corcoran have will still follow and come after me now that I'm out."

Sid shared more recent paranoia and hallucinations. "The TV on the bus told me I was supposed to be infiltrating the military. I was real manicy a month ago, and I set my jacket on fire. I set a lot of what I owned on fire then.

"I went to court for the fire because I scorched part of a wall. I have to appear back for a hearing on this case in a month. They want to put me in jail for 90 days for this, but the public defender wants me to go to trial on it."

This is a clear example of how quickly the disturbed behavior of mentally ill people becomes criminalized, particularly when their prior behavior has led to incarceration.

Now that Sidney was back on his meds he seemed to be struggling more successfully with his turmoil. He informed me he has a new outpatient team of a psychiatrist and psychologist who come to his home on a regular basis, and he is beginning to trust them. He shared his ambivalence about taking medication. "They tell me I look and act better and present myself better in public, and I'm not a danger to myself and others when I'm on meds. But I feel my brain cramp up when I take them, and I don't articulate well. When I stop meds, I feel more motivated, more purpose-driven. I will break a leg to get things done."

At this point, he shared a startling revelation that was crucial to understanding why he had so often refused his meds in the past. "My brother died in 2005 from a bad medication reaction while in a mental hospital. Just like I feared they were doing to me!" I wondered if the prison psychiatrists knew this crucial fact. I never saw any evidence they were aware of it in his corrections medical file.

All antipsychotic meds have serious side effects. The most serious include diabetes, high cholesterol, restlessness, heat stroke, extreme fatigue, and involuntary movements of the mouth and tongue. Patients continue these necessary medications only when they have an ongoing collaborative, supportive, and trusting relationship with a psychiatrist who regularly weighs and shares with them the damaging effects of the meds against the therapeutic benefit.

I tried to get a sense of what Sidney's life was like growing up and asked about his early years. He recalled that his troubles started with fights in preschool and continued throughout his education. He was sent home for "cussing out a teacher." He never knew his father, and the only thing he remembers about him is his name. "Sometimes," he reflected, "I even forget that."

His mom supported the family by being a caregiver. When he was 12 years old, he told her he felt he could fly like Superman. He was placed on his first psychiatric medication, the activating antidepressant Welbutrin, for moodiness at the age of 13. At that same age he began to smoke weed and drink alcohol. By age 18, he was using methamphetamine regularly. Later, he drank a lot more and snorted heroin. He claimed speed didn't make him paranoid, but calmed him down.

He shared with pride that when he played football in his senior year of high school he was in the newspapers when he recovered a fumble and also when he made a great tackle. He had a girlfriend in high school for a month and another later for three months, but his last relationship was in 2009 for less than two weeks, because he hadn't been out of jail for more than three months since then.

Sidney described a strong genetic predisposition to mental illness. Two younger sisters are bipolar and on medication. He also has a maternal aunt who is bi-polar and a grandmother who may be manic. As he put it, "She moves around a lot, like me and my sisters."

2001 was a critical year for him. "I was in my first mental hospital, my first jail, and took my first mood stabilizer that year. A psychiatrist put me on 1500 mg of Depakote [a mood stabilizer that prevents sei-zures], and I had a seizure. I've been on and off meds since then. When they gave me Thorazine with the Depakote, I got all locked up. I'll fight any psychia-trist who puts me on that."

Since I had prescribed that combination in the dis-tant past, I felt a mild tinge of anxiety and guilt in response to his comment.

Sid was subdued during our contact, almost de-pressed. I felt this was undoubtedly related to his cousin's recent death, a connection I proposed to him.

He responded, "The only thing keeping me back from anger is that him and my brother are both in a good place now."

I asked him about suicidal thoughts and actions. He answered, "I have the thoughts, but I tell myself I won't even do it when I have that feeling. I've OD'd a few times and shot myself in 2010. That was the last time. After that I told myself I'd never do it."

Sidney still has delusions and hallucinations simi-lar to those previously described, but they were not as tortured or frightening. I asked if he'd had any hallucinations during the time he was with me. He replied he'd had one but wouldn't share it because it was "real personal."

Toward the end of our interview, Sidney asked me how he could cope with the voices and visions. This question is a crucial one for individuals with psychotic symptoms to ask their psychotherapist, because it opens the door to their learning cognitive-behavioral techniques for dealing with the relationship between inner turmoil and troubling hallucinations. I told him this was a great question that could lead to a meaningful dialogue with his therapist, although I felt an urge to begin to teach him the techniques right then. I would have exceeded the boundaries of my relationship with him to attempt therapy in our one-session meeting. His next response told me my answer to his question missed the mark for him.

"The psychiatrists and psychologists keep asking the same questions over and over, and I never get to learn how to control the voices."

I urged him to ask his present therapy team to help him with this. I shook hands and chatted with the mourning family, who were still in the lobby when I left. Sid looked down, then straight up at me and said, "I think I'll ask the psychiatrist for more meds when I see him next week." His affirmation led me to feel he'd finally heard how critical it was for him to take his medication. More importantly, he was beginning to build a trusting relationship with his new outpatient therapeutic team. This helped me feel more secure about turning him back to his treatment providers now that I was leaving him.

CHAPTER 4

Cross-Examination of a California Prison Psychiatrist

———

I WAS APPALLED BY THE psychiatrist's treatment of Sidney as described in the preceding chapter, as well as the doctor's lack of direct involvement in the extraction I watched. I tried to remain open-minded and curious as to how Dr. X, as I have called him, would describe his version of the treatment, cell extraction, and restraints in federal court. A meticulous cross-examination followed his testimony, conducted by an attorney who I will call Libby, employed by the firm representing the inmates in the Coleman suit.

Dr. X was the psychiatrist on the crisis unit where Sidney was housed during the twenty-four days before the cell extraction. He cited Sidney's gradual deterioration during that time, testifying to his patient's becoming progressively more bizarre and noncommunicative. He confirmed that the cell was flooded with water, urine and feces at the time of the extraction. Finally, Dr. X decided Sidney was sufficiently disabled to warrant involuntary medication. He ordered the extraction because he thought it was the only means at his disposal to get Sidney to take the meds. His recollection was that his patient was only sprayed twice, and not the seven times I had observed on the tape.

He stated that despite being gravely disabled, Sidney was among a group of psychotic patients able to comprehend the order to "cuff up" and have the mental faculties to choose to refuse to do so. This was Dr. X's contention even though the officer who supervised the extraction stated Sidney's mental confusion was so severe he was unable "to follow the simplest instruction."

Dr. X.'s view of the takedown was, "He was flailing and very resistant. They secured control of him only after he had to be taken to the ground, and officers were on every limb."

In my view, the lack of understanding on the part of the officers and psychiatrist of Sidney's confusion and why the brutal extraction was so threatening to him resulted in an escalation of a struggle that in the end required at least an officer on every limb to restrain him.

Libby, Sidney's attorney, established from the medical record that his existing treatment plan and institutional guidelines had called for him to be transferred to a higher level of psychiatric care after ten days of not responding.

However, Dr. X had chosen not to transfer Sidney after the ten days of his not responding to treatment. Libby followed up by asking, "So it is your opinion, when you're treating patients in your crisis bed unit, that you can help them more by keeping them while they deteriorate in order to get them eventually on involuntary medications."

Dr. X didn't recognize how self-indicting it was when he replied, "Exactly." It's significant that he never filled out the paperwork to complete the request for legal involuntary medication, which he could have done the first day he thought it was necessary.

Libby also established that Dr. X had ordered Sidney back to his cell in administrative segregation after sixteen days, but later rescinded the order. In response to her query about his reasons for ordering the discharge, he stated, "It was obvious we weren't being effective. We weren't doing anything. . . In my opinion he could sit in his cell outside of that unit and deteriorate, which seemed to me to be inevitable."

The inmate's attorney followed up with, "So in your opinion at that time it was preferable to discharge him back to an EOP administrative segregation unit

[Ad Seg] where he would sit in the cell and deteriorate than refer him to a higher level of care for treatment?"

Dr. X answered simply, "Yes."

EOP is the acronym for enhanced outpatient program. This is the highest level of psychiatric treatment available within the California correctional system outside of a mental-health crisis bed. It is a gross misnomer, as all too often the care at this level falls way below even correctional standards for mental-health care. This is even more the case when "treatment" occurs in an Ad Seg unit, which is a current euphemism for solitary confinement. Only the secure housing unit or SHU exceeds it in lack of social and environmental stimulation. Mentally ill inmates were also kept in the SHU prior to the most recent Coleman lawsuit, which was partially successful in limiting use of Ad Seg and SHU for the psychiatrically disabled.

Dr. X maintained Sidney in restraints continuously for 72 hours. This is an outrageously long time to keep a patient throttled. In order to do so, X had to justify the need for this level of constraint and renew the order every four hours.

After many injections of powerful antipsychotic meds, Sidney did finally calm down and began to politely and calmly ask to be taken out of restraints. Dr. X repeatedly refused to do so because, he said, "Sidney would not acknowledge and state the reason he's restrained. He claims he doesn't remember what happened yesterday, which is untrue. Acutely psychotic people remember events very well."

In my own clinical experience, severely disturbed patients often do not remember their psychotic behaviors because to do so would be further traumatizing to their fragile egos. However, recall is not the issue here. What limited Sidney's ability to explain why he was extracted and restrained was his experience of these procedures as unexplainable murderous assault.

The next day Sidney "softly" apologized to Dr. X and asked what he would have to do to get himself released. X replied with the same verbal response he had written on his progress note. "If you cannot remember what you'd have to do, then you certainly are not appropriate for release."

Dr. X's progress note continued, "Patient broke off conversation. Appeared to be seething. Five-point restraints continued."

This prison psychiatrist was asking a patient whom he designated as gravely disabled and in a paranoid psychosis to answer a question he did not understand in order to get out of a torturously extensive period of severe restraint. He provoked the patient's anger by demanding an answer to a question Sidney could not comprehend let alone answer, and then interpreted his anger as evidence he was not ready to be taken out of restraints.

Finally, another psychiatrist was on duty the morning of Sidney's fourth strapped-down day and released him from restraints. I wonder how much longer Sidney would have been remained in restraints if Dr. X hadn't taken a day off.

I am very aware of the many realities to any occurrence, especially in prisons. However, in reading the transcript of the doctor's testimony, I can certainly understand why Sidney deteriorated and was not willing to cooperate with Dr. X. It easy to see the role X had in escalating Sidney's psychosis and misunderstanding him, then maintaining him in restraints for three days and permitting harsh punishment for his psychotic behaviors.

The same attorney who examined him in the preceding court case deposed Dr. X again in October 2015. This was in response to a civil suit Sydney filed concerning the psychological damage done to him as a result of his care and cell extraction while in CDCR. In this deposition, X described a lack of professionalism even more outlandish than that in the previous use-of-force case.

Dr. X reported he had been fired from one state prison, allegedly for not evaluating the suicidal potential of every patient. Shortly afterward, he was hired to work at Corcoran. About four years after he started at Corcoran, and shortly after the cell extraction described above, Corcoran terminated Dr. X.

Included in his reasons for ordering extractions in general was the "patient becoming unhappy with the questions I am asking." I could certainly understand why patients were unhappy with his questions, as several of his queries to Sidney were quite provocative. His main reason for not referring patients who needed it to acute care was "because primarily, number one, it required a lot of paperwork." He did also acknowledge an institutional issue—the great delays and many difficulties in transferring patients—but number one was his avoidance of paperwork. And he readily admitted it in a formal deposition.

He said he recommended that Sidney be transferred out of a mental-health crisis bed because "We weren't doing anything" and "All we are doing is keeping records." Dr. X said he didn't fill out an application for involuntary meds until about ten days after the team decided it was necessary "because we were determining who would do it."

He also cited resistance on the part of judges to grant involuntary medication and gave the example of a judge who said fecal smearing wasn't necessarily psychosis, that it could potentially be art with feces being the only material available to an inmate in solitary.

There are apparently a number of incompetent physicians in the California prison system. According to an *L.A. Times* article in July 2011, California prisons have a record of employing troubled doctors, and 20 percent to 50 percent of physicians provide poor-quality care. Many have had their medical license suspended for years. Dozens of inadequate doctors are not fired but paid over $250,000 annually to stay away from patients and shuffle papers in what is known as "mailroom" duty.

Of course, many good clinicians provide mental-health services in California correctional systems as well. A skilled prison psychiatrist is described in the following chapter. My hope is for the creation of a therapeutic environment where competent physicians and therapists don't give up and leave or burn out. Not only can well-trained clinicians understand and treat the roots of disturbed behaviors, they can also train correctional staff to comprehend and manage them as well.

CHAPTER 5

A Reasonable Prison Psychiatrist

A FORMER TRAINEE OF MINE has been intermittently working in the California state prison system for nearly a decade. During my 2013-14 evaluations for the Coleman suit, I visited two institutions where he had worked. The psychiatrists at both facilities spoke very highly of him and hoped he would return, which in fact had occurred when I spoke with him in early summer of 2015. I often wondered why he chose to work in this system, as he had many other opportunities. Dr. K., as I will refer to him, had come back for several practical reasons. He had previous state service and hoped to be vested in the pension program in a few more years. His opinion was that many of the other psychiatrists stayed because each year brought another 2.5 percent of maximum salary to their pension. He acknowledged that salaries had improved in the state prisons as a direct result of the Coleman suit.

Dr. K. preferred the daily prison work schedule of 7:30 a.m. to 3:30 p.m. to the hours required in private practice, which had extended into the late evening. He enjoyed being with his family after work when he was not being besieged with phone calls or catching up with pre-authorizations and other paperwork. He was relieved to be away from the politics and infighting of academic psychiatry, and the ethics of research and talks for "Big Pharma."

But he paid a price. He addressed several major problems associated with working in the state prisons: the lack of respect for psychiatrists, the working conditions, the relationship with and structure of custody, and the lack of any consistent therapeutic approach.

"In this system, mental-health staff gets identified with their patients and are treated not unlike prisoners," Dr. K. said. "Most of the chief psychiatrist positions are unfilled or have been eliminated. This has left the psychologists with more power in the system than the psychiatrists. The role of psychiatry has shrunk to being a medication vending machine. Not that they use psychologists well, either, and they employ massive numbers of them. But most of them truly could not find work elsewhere. Furthermore, I report to a physician who is a surgeon and has no certification in psychiatry."

"The real problem is the working conditions," he continued. "The office space is tiny and toxic. There is no meaningful therapy for patients, only medications—and only for the severest of illnesses. There is no licensed acute care, no medical staff organization, only limited, non-progressive medical care. There is a shortage of crisis beds, so they bus the convicts all over the state trying to find an appropriate bed. Suicidal inmates in transit spend their nights in a cage. It takes one or two days for them to get their meds when they finally arrive at the new facility."

K sighed before continuing, "Most evaluations are oriented toward blaming the patient rather than considering how to help. Sometimes I spend an hour a day walking patients from their cells to my office and back. At least because of the Coleman Case I can do therapy in a confidential space and not outside of a cell door. But because of Coleman I now have to spend a lot of time transferring unnecessary data from one place to another in the inmates' records."

Dr. K shed new light on the issue of custody's relationship with treatment: "The custodial environment is regressive, unenlightened, and really just warehousing as economically as possible. The system is punitive to staff, responding only to needs when a crisis erupts. With all the changes that have been made and higher salaries for mental health, the former custodial infrastructure is still there. They have not changed the personnel or the management. The system is filled with 'experts,' 'know-it-alls,' and those with strong political agendas. Mental health is at the bottom of this pecking order."

The prison system has not created a workable hierarchy, Dr. K said. "The old guard is still there with the same attitude and inefficiency. For example, at one facility they created an attempt at a therapy environment where the inmate would be behind a glass wall and the therapist would speak to the patient through an intercom. They spent six months trying to get the intercom to work, and never did it function."

I wondered how Dr. K. coped with the frustrations he'd expressed.

He responded, "I meditate. I backpack for weeks at a time. Another advantage of this type of work. I speak up quite a bit and things get a little better, but it's tricky. I do want to say that working with the patients is my mission there. I feel I can do something with them. I don't even mind seeing them in a cage if that's the only way they will let me see my patients."

Dr. K. is not the only state prison psychiatrist who acknowledges the problems with this system. A former chief psychiatrist and medical director at San Quentin State Prison, complained bitterly about mental-health care within the state system. "Dozens of patients who required acute inpatient psychiatric care at San Quentin were . . . restricted from or totally deprived of access within the 136 million-dollar health-care facility recently opened in 2010," he said. "Instead," he added, "these patients, suffering from acute episodes of mental illness, were held in improper, temporary overflow cells where they would often wait for several days [until] delivered to vacant beds . . . at distant institutions."

This former San Quentin psychiatrist attacked the department's medical plan as not only unnecessary but also "dangerous to patients . . . the public, and prison staff." He wrote in a March 2014 memo that conditions then were constitutionally inadequate and that the psychologist chief of mental health there had a lengthy track record of mistreating psychologists as well as psychiatrists." He also claimed he was menaced and harassed for fourteen months after he sent his original memo and that he was threatened with being fired or transferred to a prison "in the middle of the desert" and coerced to resign as chief psychiatrist.

Not surprisingly, psychologists are also critics of the system. A psychologist at one of the more antiquated prisons I visited took me aside and shared, "The only way they could ever deliver mental-health care here would be if they blew the place up and started all over."

CHAPTER 6

Anatomy of a Prison Suicide

AUGUST 9, 2013. A 60-YEAR-OLD inmate in administrative segregation at Mule Creek State Prison in California hung and killed himself at 1:50 in the afternoon. Peter, as I will call him, tied one end of a sheet to the top of an upper bunk frame and the other end into a noose, which he placed around his neck, and then jumped.

His limp body was not found until several hours after he hung himself, but immediately after discovery three officers rushed to his cell. The first charged in, thrusting forward a heavy, full-body shield. A second placed the dead man in handcuffs. Finally, the third cut the noose away from the bed and all three "gently" lowered him to the floor, slid him out of the cell, and placed him in leg shackles. Only after Peter was bound hand and foot did efforts to revive him begin. CPR, intubation and three injections of epinephrine were all unsuccessful. He was pronounced dead a half hour later.

I had a flash of understanding when I read of this sequence. How frightened for their own safety the officers must have been to protect themselves from a man who so obviously appeared to have already left this world.

Although I never met Peter, I was able to review his life history as described in prison records. He was raised in San Francisco, the eldest of four children. He did not graduate from high school but did earn a GED. He attended community college for a year and worked as a printer for four years.

In 1984, he began to believe his neighbors were spreading rumors about him, saying he was a drug dealer, and that he ate and smelled of dog feces. He believed his neighbors were planning to kill him. We know little of the course of his paranoia or his history until April 1, 1990, a day when Peter was listening to loud music in his parked car.

A woman approached and asked him to turn the music down. He thought she was involved in a conspiracy he had constructed in his mind and became angry with her, although he did not harm her. Shortly after this confrontation a male neighbor went to his car to get his tools, and Peter perceived a hammer the man was holding as a direct attack on himself and another aspect of the plot against him. Peter rushed out of his car and shot the man in the arm.

In turn, the wounded man's 60-year-old mother ran out of her house and screamed at Peter for shooting her son. Peter then pointed his gun at her. She attempted to run away but tripped and fell. He shot her in the head and started to walk away, but turned around and shot her again. After his arrest he admitted he had committed another murder a month earlier because he perceived a man had threatened to blow his head off.

Peter was taken to a county jail, where he was quickly placed on one of the early antipsychotic medications, Mellaril. This was his first known contact with mental-health treatment. (Twenty years later, Mellaril was withdrawn worldwide because of toxicity to the heart and retina.)

Peter was evaluated at Atascadero State Hospital for one year while awaiting disposition of his case. He was deemed able to stand trial and found guilty of murder in the first degree, despite his diagnosis of paranoid schizophrenia. This punitive sentencing of the mentally ill is typical of the manner in which individuals with severe psychiatric illness are evaluated by our current forensic system. This may be in part because there are so few psychiatric hospitals outside of prisons capable of handling them.

Peter was placed on monthly injections of long-acting Haldol until he was switched to Risperdal by mouth. Both of these are newer antipsychotics with fewer side effects than Mellaril. He stayed on Risperdal for eighteen years and did reasonably well on this medication. He was able to work content-edly in a prison shoe factory despite the presence of continued delusions of persecution that intensified intermittently.

A woman he considered his 'long-term' girlfriend died during his prolonged incarceration, and after this loss he annually mourned the anniversary of her death. Unfortunately in 2001 his delusions worsened, focusing on fears other inmates were spreading rumors about him that would get him killed. He was placed in segregation "for his own protection."

Here, as is often the case with psychotic inmates, he became more agitated and delusional. The sensory deprivation of Ad Seg outweighed any sense of security he might have felt there. He accused inmates of saying he "smelled like shit." He also complained about his cellmates because they smelled and were mentally ill. He was eventually granted a single cell. All too often inmates whose mental illness makes it impossible for them to have a roommate are punished severely for refusing a "cellie." They are considered to be disobedient rather than frightened or ill. In this instance, it appears his paranoia was sufficiently recognizable that he was not punished for his request.

Peter became obsessively focused on his parole hearing, approaching it with irrational optimism. After being denied parole in 2009 he developed new symptoms, including rapid swings between hopeless despair and upbeat optimism. He felt that taking Risperdal was preventing him from being paroled, so he asked to have it discontinued. The antipsychotic medication was gradually tapered over a year and stopped in November 2012. When patients are taken off these meds after decades, they need to be carefully monitored for at least their first drug-free year.

He was transferred from CDCR's California Medical Facility to Folsom State Prison in May 2013. A suicide assessment performed at this facility did not pick up his emerging suicidal thoughts. A psychiatrist who later evaluated this assessment found it "incomplete and inaccurate." By this time, Peter was totally off his medications, deteriorating, and threatening to kill anyone who showed him ill will. He wanted to "separate their souls from their bodies." He also felt inmates were spreading rumors he "had been charged with a sex crime." He began to feel he had special abilities to do extraordinary acts and heard "voices all around him."

Two psychiatrists evaluated him for involuntary medications. I was shocked by their conclusion that he did not even meet criteria for a court hearing to assess this possibility. A plan was developed to transfer him to a facility where he could get intensive therapy, but instead he was transferred to Mule Creek State Prison. How could this mistake have happened? A more therapeutic environment could have saved his life. But mistakes like this are often made in our jails and prisons.

Mule Creek staff changed his diagnosis from schizophrenia to major depression. But regardless of the name of his illness, there was little treatment available. Incongruent with his new diagnosis, he was now having delusions that inmates and officers were out to pummel him with hammers and kill him, and that he had super powers. Individuals who are depressed may have delusions their body is rotting or the world is ending, but generally not grandiose ideas such as having super powers.

Peter had entered CDCR free of medical conditions. By the time he was transferred to Mule Creek, he had developed: type 2 diabetes, high cholesterol, glaucoma, peripheral neuropathy, anemia, and arthritis. The first two conditions quite possibly were caused by the medications that had controlled his psychosis. However, multiple severe medical complications are quite common among older inmates, even those who are not mentally ill.

In July 2013, his mental-health treatment team decided a transfer back to a mental-health unit was not indicated. On August 8, a psychiatrist decided Peter still did not meet criteria for involuntary meds even though he continued to believe everyone was talking about him and wanted to kill him.

During the last weeks of his life, Peter often asked to see a mental-health clinician, but there is no evidence this took place. One request for this help was poignantly worded: "I tried to tell you long before this got to be such a critical mess." His potential for suicide had been evaluated multiple times, and no chronic or acute factors were found until June of 2013. At that time chronic risk was rated moderate, but acute risk was still rated low. It is hard to believe so many indicators for suicide were there, yet missed. I can only speculate that this is either because so many inmates talk about suicide so often that their pleas for help are ignored, or their evaluators have become indifferent.

On the morning of the day he died, Peter was at his cell door screaming, "An inmate killed my family and raped my sister!" He accused another inmate of raping him through the cell wall. A female corrections sergeant said to him, "That must have hurt." He was quite agitated that morning, but corrections evaluated his level of disturbance as "not more than usual," so no mental-health referral was initiated. A few hours after he began his latest desperate plea for help, Peter hung himself.

Many deceased inmates in Ad Seg have not been found until after rigor mortis has set in. Yet CDCR continues to keep mentally disturbed inmates in segregation and refuses to have staggered frequent checks for all inmates so housed, which could prevent many suicides. Even inmates who enter segregation without psychiatric problems are vulnerable to suicide in segregation. It is difficult enough for "sane" inmates to be in seclusion. I can't imagine how a mentally ill person can handle a prolonged stay in such deprivation.

California prisons average 24 suicides per 100,000 inmates, the second highest rate in the USA. The incidence of suicides in CDCR is 48 percent higher than the national state prison average, and inmates in segregation are 33 times more likely to suicide than those in general population.

Even though the rate of suicide in California prisons is shockingly high, it is half the overall rate of local jails in the nation. Local jails have high suicide rates because of inadequate time to assess inmates, rapid turnover, the immediacy of apprehension and untreated addiction and acute mental illness. This is another reason why the mass release of state prison inmates to city and county jails is not a long-term solution for the psychological problems of the incarcerated mentally ill. The high suicide rate in CDCR has continued to occur despite twenty years of litigation and federal monitoring meant to pressure corrections to stop violating the rights of the mentally ill, inflicting cruel and inhumane punishment, and precipitating astounding rates of suicide.

Two-thirds of California prison suicide victims have been previously identified as mentally ill, yet screening and treatment remain almost absent in Ad Seg. Here, inmates who have not violated any regulations spend 23 hours a day for years, even decades, in cramped cells with little if any sensory stimulation or human contact.

These circumstances lead them to become actively suicidal even if they never contemplated taking their life prior to being placed in seclusion. When therapy is available, it takes place at cell front or in cages with hands and feet shackled. Still, corrections can say that therapy is offered, even though inmates so often refuse it because of the conditions that go along with it.

The glaring but sad evidence that correctional authorities have not dealt with the conditions leading to inmate suicide is the continued rate of self-annihilation among mentally ill inmates. In 2013, there were

30 suicides in CDCR. In the first seven months of 2014, 11 of 14 suicides took place in solitary. Ten of these eleven inmates were designated mentally ill. Yet, Corrections continues to claim it is improving mental-health care and suicide prevention.

Dr. Lindsay Hayes, a national expert on suicide in prison, was hired directly by CDCR to evaluate the inmate suicide problem and make recommendations to reduce the number of suicides. He found the conditions suicidal inmates faced in 2011 similar to those I reported. Hayes found that potentially suicidal inmates were kept in dim, dirty, airless cells with unsanitized mattresses on the floor. He reviewed 25 case histories of suicides and found seven who had killed themselves within hours or days of being released from suicide watch. CPR was not attempted in 68 percent of these fatalities. Guards, not mental-health workers, dictated all conditions of the suicide watch and falsified logs showing how often inmates were checked as was documented in the Coleman suit.

Dr. Hayes warned that punitive and anti-therapeutic suicide watch practices encouraged inmates to kill themselves. He suggested stopping harsh tactics like withholding showers and stripping inmates naked, and implementing careful tracking of those who have attempted suicide. His report was released in

August 2011, and few if any of the recommendations were followed.

Hayes complained about the lack of responsiveness to his findings, and his three-year consulting contract was suddenly canceled. The corrections department's suicide coordinator wrote to Hayes in June 2012, "Obviously, when your report landed it was not roundly applauded and in fact was buried." Corrections asked Hayes to remove the damaging findings from his report, and he complied. However, inmate attorneys obtained a complete copy and a federal judge overruled the state's attempts to squelch the complete evaluation.

The Special Master who reviewed CDCR's compliance with the court-ordered conditions of the initial Coleman settlement has appointed six mental-health experts as his evaluators. They have been assessing mental health care since 1999, and a key aspect of their job has been to review the problem of prison suicides. One of the experts, Raymond Patterson, has been focusing on this problem. Patterson stated that CDCR's review process for evaluating suicides improved during the first few years of his observation. However, for the last ten years of his tenure, he experienced increasing frustration because year after year, his repeated recommendations were not utilized.

In his final report, based on a review of the data and a comprehensive review of 15 cases of suicide that took place in the first six months of 2012, Patterson noted the following:

a. The suicide rate has rapidly increased from 2005 to 2012.
b. In one-fifth of cases, the body was not discovered till two to four hours after death
c. In 87 percent of reviewed suicides, there was some degree of inadequacy in evaluation of suicide risk, treatment, or clinical intervention.
d. 73 percent of suicides were either foreseeable or preventable.

Dr. Patterson's recommendations, which were repeatedly ignored, included:

a. Follow existing guidelines for delivery of mental-health services.
b. Fully implement suicide review and other review processes already in place.
c. Monitor and assess suicidal inmates more closely.
d. Refer decompensating suicidal inmates to Department of Mental Health facilities.

Dr. Raymond Patterson resigned in March 2013, stating that his recommendations went "unheeded year after year" while suicides "go unabated" and that any further recommendations would be "a waste of time and effort."

When I conducted my own review of the suicide problem in CDCR, I discovered that an excellent mental-health protocol was in place for evaluating suicidal individuals. The format even involved forming an empathic relationship with the patient before an assessment of suicidal potential took place. The prison psychiatrist I spoke with about this protocol evaluated potential suicidal individuals every day. He had never heard of this program or been assessed as to his ability to empathize and bring other relationship-building techniques into his evaluation.

This is not an unusual phenomenon in corrections—detailed policy and procedures with no related action. New policies for responding to suicidal threats may help for the moment, but they do not get to the root of the problem.

The problem is overcrowded, decadent treatment facilities staffed by unhappy mental-health workers who are dominated by frightened, angry custodial officers. It is difficult enough for sane inmates to survive in these conditions, let alone those who are mentally ill.

Sometimes I wonder if there is not a latent or perhaps even overt wish on the part of custody staff that these difficult, psychotic and/or suicidal inmates disappear by whatever means possible.

Peter's problem, like those of many of the other severely disturbed inmates in our country's jails and prisons, is a desperate conundrum. He was certainly way beyond the level of mental illness any penal institution could and should handle. Yet he killed two people, which places him well above the potential for violence that psychiatric hospitals can cope with. Peter and others with his degree of illness require specialized care in which treatment and custody are at parallel hierarchies and work as a team. That is the only system under which inmate patients like him have a chance to recover or even to survive.

Because of a legal technicality, the circumstances of the tragedy of Peter's suicide were not presented in the federal court that evaluated mental-health care in segregation in California prisons. This chapter represents the only public hearing of the tragedy of Peter's suicide.

CHAPTER 7

The Judge Enters the Fray

In November 2013, I testified before a federal judge on the use of segregation for mentally ill offenders in California state prisons. The hearing took place in a modern courthouse in Sacramento the week before Thanksgiving.

The female attorney who represented these inmates was a bright, compassionate Yale law graduate dedicated to social justice. We had visited three state prisons together, and also reviewed the medical and custodial records of many inmates with mental illness. She was deeply moved by the horrible ways these prisoners were treated. She fought off tears and managed to hold herself together during our interviews but broke down and sobbed after an inmate who had attempted suicide many times had left the room. I prepared a 160-page report on my findings, and she memorized every word for my pretrial deposition.

Rather than quote statistics, we agreed to focus my testimony on the history of five inmates, each of whom demonstrated a glaring deficiency in mental-health care.

The CDCR attorneys struck down our presentation of the tragic suicide of the inmate described in the preceding chapter. The defense argued that the suicide was only a few months before this trial, and they had no time to prepare their defense. The judge upheld their objection.

Everyone in every courtroom I have ever been in has been asked to stand in respect whenever a judge is about to enter, and federal courtrooms are the most formal. However, as soon as Judge Lawrence Karlton appeared, he dismissively waved us to sit back down immediately. This scenario was repeated each time he entered. Nevertheless, a federal judge has a godlike quality. Even his beard was longer and whiter than my own.

A classic courtroom scenario evolved, with each side attempting to prove its points as skillfully and aggressively as possible. What was different in this trial, which did not involve a jury, were my conversations with the judge. He huffed and sighed impatiently at the way both sets of lawyers queried me. He often confronted the attorneys on each side, and then asked me a direct question that led to a dialogue. I felt like there was no one in the room but the two of us. My attitude rapidly shifted from compliance or combat with the attorneys to just being myself. The tone of my voice even became conversational. I continued to feel valued whenever he asked me a direct question.

The first time the judge and I spoke directly, he asked my opinion on putting a suicidal inmate in what the inmates' lawyers referred to as a "cage" and CDCR called a "therapeutic module." I mentioned both terms in my testimony so as not to appear biased, but it looked and felt like a cruel and inhumane cage to me, barely suitable for an outraged wild animal.

My dialogue with the judge, which follows, is edited to avoid the run-on sentences, repetitions and glaring grammatical errors typical of courtroom exchanges as accurately recorded by stenographers. My thoughts and comments are in italics. In the official transcript, the judge is referred to as "THE COURT," and I am "THE WITNESS."

THE COURT: "Do you realize that custody has placed the inmate in a therapeutic module to handle an acute crisis and not a long-term problem?"

THE WITNESS: "I do. And I realize the immediate need is to have the inmate be safe. And that's ostensibly the reason why the inmate is handled in this way. But many, if not most, if not all the inmates I talked to felt degraded whenever they expressed suicidal ideation. If they dared to mention it, they were bound hand and foot, and put in a cage."

I paused, then continued: "In the outside psychiatric world we don't treat human beings that way. If they are suicidal, we form an empathic relationship first. If absolutely necessary, we place them in a setting where we have what we call one-on-one observation, where staff is within arm's length of them all the time to provide care as well as structure. In custody, a trained fellow inmate can perform this function quite well. Or we put them in safety cells, where they can't hurt themselves and are observed constantly.

"But for all the inmates I spoke to, being caged was degrading and dehumanizing. Many of them shared with me [that] they hesitated to speak about their suicidal ideas with custody or mental-health staff because they feared the brutal way their pain would be responded to."

A few minutes later, I again turned to the judge when he asked, "In a prison system as huge as California's, is it practical to evaluate each inmate efficiently and sensibly?"

THE WITNESS: "It would be if conditions were different. Over half the psychologists were on prolonged sick leave at one of the prisons I visited. There is an extreme shortage of psychiatrists throughout the system. If you have insufficient staff, then you can't do it. The reason people go out on prolonged sick leave and that it is so hard to get psychiatrists is because of the working conditions, the lack of the barest minimum of a therapeutic environment. How can you get psychotherapists to work in a system where they are expected to perform group or individual therapy with patients shackled hand and foot in a cage?"

THE COURT: "Your view, as I hear what you have just said, which is new, is that, look, part of the reality of the difficulty recruiting adequate mental-health providers is nobody wants to work in—not nobody, very few people—are going to want to work in conditions as severe as this. Is that your view, sir?"

THE WITNESS: "Yes, it is."

THE COURT: "So the conditions themselves in your view are significant limitations in the ability to make discrete judgments about inmates. You can't get mental-health staff to work there because the conditions are so severe?"

THE WITNESS: "That's part of it. But another frequent occurrence is that mental-health staff sometimes gets co-opted by custody, so they, too, become more concerned with custodial issues than what is therapeutic or humane.

"On the other hand, other mental-health personnel often get frustrated arguing with custody for a treatment-oriented environment for inmates, and they give up or burn out. And then they go out on extended sick leave, or they, too, become more custody-oriented in their approach.

"If I go back to the many disciplinary reports I reviewed in the use-of-force case [*another trial earlier that year with the same judge*], I saw how often a mental-health worker made a recommendation that an inmate's mental illness contributed to his alleged "crime" within the prison—and yet the individual lost thirty, sixty, days, three hundred sixty-five days of earned good time for an infraction like refusing medications that have side effects or for psychotic fecal smearing.

"You stop feeling your contributions make a difference to the care of the inmates, and so you give up and burn out."

THE COURT: "Setting aside those folks who just give up and burn out and so forth, I have always been puzzled about who would be willing to be a psychologist or psychiatrist in a prison. The lawyers have heard me say that you've got to be crazy to want to work in one of those places, but as a serious matter, even people who would be willing to do so, for a variety of reasons that human beings are willing to do difficult work, your view, I take it, is that individualized assessments of prisoners to determine what level of security is necessary are simply defeated by the very nature of the conditions in which the prisoners are being treated? Is that fair?"

THE WITNESS: "It is. But it still could be done. Some of the clinicians I talked to were excellent and well-trained. Given better conditions and more authority, these people could do a decent assessment."

THE COURT: "If I ever get to writing this ruling, I want to be clear that you are saying that the punitive aspects of security themselves result in many people not wanting to work in these prisons. These extreme conditions limit the real-world ability to have adequate assessments even when there are individual physicians or psychologists who would be willing and able. In your view, is the difficulty recruiting and retaining professionals affected by the severity of the conditions as you see them?"

THE WITNESS: "Absolutely."

THE COURT: "Thank you."

Another key critique I had of the system was termed "second return" or "psych and return." We used this term to describe a common problem where an inmate decompensates in segregation, is moved to a mental-health crisis bed and recovers in a week or two. As soon as he is better, he is transferred back to the environment that had a significant role in his psychotic behavior or suicidal drive.

The CDCR attorney challenged me immediately after I gave several examples of this problem but was rapidly put in his place by the judge, who scolded: "I have no idea what you are talking about. The objection is that he's returning to the precise place that contributed to his being moved to a mental-health bed. Objection overruled!"

THE COURT: "Doctor, you mentioned several times the security provisions employed. I don't really understand what you are saying when you say, "I've done this for 50 years; I have never had to shackle or cage inmates before." Have you treated patients in security housing units before or administrative segregation units?"

THE WITNESS: "I set up programs in the New York City prison system for inmates that were in those levels of housing. When I was in the Lewisburg Federal Penitentiary as chief of psychiatric services, I led group therapy in my office in the prison hospital. Everyone sat in a chair without hand- or leg cuffs."

THE COURT: "I want to go back to something I've inquired about from one of your other experts. I mean, we begin with these are prisons. These are people who have disobeyed society's standards. That's why they are there. But yet, many of them are in segregation because there is no appropriate bed. What I hear you saying, and what I heard the other expert say yesterday, seems to suggest that there should be, at least at minimum, a more refined examination of the prisoner before his treatment is so restricted."

Judge Karlton had answered his own question with his statement, so we proceeded to the morning break, introduced by the judge with, "I'm about to get scolded by my courtroom reporter. We'll take morning recess now."

I realized then that even federal judges have to answer to someone.

A few hours on a witness stand, even as an expert, are exhausting and emotionally draining. At this point I was looking forward to a break and re-strategizing with the inmates' team of five expert attorneys.

Shortly after the recess, the judge interrupted and took over again. The prisoners' rights attorney had asked me why a hallucinating schizophrenic woman needed a high level of mental-health treatment. As I started my sentence with, "Well, because as I've said . . .," the judge interrupted me with his obvious agreement, "They're sick!"

I continued to testify about how destructive segregated housing is to mentally ill inmates, including the high rate of suicide in these settings. The judge responded with genuine interest and an attentive facial expression.

THE COURT: "Doctor, what are you going to do? These folks may be mentally ill, but they're in a prison, and prisons require relatively strict rules. These people will apparently consistently violate those rules. What are the prison officials supposed to do?"

THE WITNESS: "Most of their rule violations are because of their mental illness.

When inmates smear feces on themselves and their cell walls because they're extremely psychotic, you don't take sixty days' good time away from them, for instance. You look at this behavior as a symptom of severe mental illness.

"But to answer your question as to what to do, you need a specialized kind of facility to treat these individuals, and then you need something that doesn't seem to exist in CDCR. You need a therapeutic unit with a gradual step down so that inmates see there's a way out of segregation or other specialized units. One aspect of a step down is providing hope, because part of the trauma of being in the SHU *[secure housing unit, formerly called solitary confinement]* for thirteen years, like one of the inmate patients I interviewed, is losing the belief you will ever get out. That's absolutely essential, but also a step-down can be very therapeutic.

"You say to somebody: 'You go to all your assigned activities and you participate. You stay out of trouble for a few weeks and open up with your therapist, and you get more privileges.' And so the step-down rewards good behavior and also rewards therapeutic work and behavioral improvement, and supports the individual becoming less dangerous to himself and others.

"You create an environment where not only can the inmate see there's a way out of the SHU, but by behaving in a progressively more appropriate way and participating in therapeutic activities, they get to feel more sane."

There were some points the judge was getting tired of hearing. When I testified how inmates were strip searched every time they left their cell, the judge interrupted me and said, "And coming back."

THE WITNESS: "And coming back again."

THE COURT: "I've only heard that at least 14 or 15 times. I mean, it is really new to me. You may proceed."

Nevertheless, I gave my opinion about this practice, explaining, "It should not be done as a routine matter. There has to be a reason to strip search. It should not be universal. It should only be performed for a clear indication or some grave demonstration of dangerous behavior."

THE COURT: "And you are expressing that opinion based as a matter of your judgment. What is your rationale or basis for that opinion?"

THE WITNESS: "Because in the majority of the cases it is unnecessary, and it results in inmates being traumatized. And it results in their refusing the therapy and other activities they desperately need."

THE COURT: "This is another one of those places in which there is a serious custody issue—sometimes you can't figure out why custody is doing the things they are doing. But this, I think, is fairly straightforward.

"Custody, as I take it, strip searches everybody because they have had experiences in which officers have been injured or people make weapons out of God knows what. So they just have a routine that says if you're in Ad Seg or any segregated housing, we're going to strip search you to be sure.

"Your view, I think, is that the harm occasioned by that practice outweighs whatever custody rationale otherwise exists. Is that fair?"

THE WITNESS: "I am very aware of the dangers to custody, of people being able to smuggle things back and forth. But particularly when an individual is in segregation because of lack of a bed, it seems to me that it is unduly punitive and anti-therapeutic to strip search them every time they enter or leave their cell—because if they were in general population, it wouldn't be done."

THE COURT: "I think this is a difficult—everything in this case is difficult, but I think this is particularly problematic. Your answer is that the proof is in the pudding, and the fact of the matter is that they would be in general population except for some reason that is not relevant to whether or not they're dangerous. Thank you. I have answered my own question."

THE WITNESS: "Exactly. Thank you."

My cross-examination by the state's counsel was relatively uneventful and resulted in little direct interaction between the judge and myself. Six hours after I started, I left the witness stand. Six months passed before the judge rendered his thoughtful decision on April 10, 2014. His decree will be summarized in a later chapter.

CHAPTER 8

Three Strikes and You're Really Out

In mid-August of 2013 I was asked by a Santa Clara public defender to evaluate William, a 45-year-old African-American man, sentenced to 78 years to life under the three-strikes law. His third strike was for cloning cell phones. His attorney was attempting to get him released after he had served 16 years, using the provisions of Proposition 36, a liberalization of the three-strikes law approved by voters in 2012.

This revision provided for resentencing and/or release of prisoners whose third offense was not serious or violent and who were not presently "unreasonable" risks to society. The three-strikes law was one of many punitive sentencing practices that led to mass incarceration.

Overcrowded prisons in turn led to diminished care and punitive practices toward all inmates, but more so toward the mentally ill. This proven fact was one of the main reasons the Coleman suit was able to greatly diminish the state prison population in California.

I entered the Santa Clara Men's Jail on a brilliantly sunny day with William's public defender at my side. He'd been transferred there to facilitate my interview. I was comforted by the attorney's presence. I had been turned away several times at the Orange County Jail under similar circumstances, despite a handful of formal approvals granting me access to interview. This jail, in contrast to most, was surprisingly easy to enter. I gave my ID at the gate and was pointed toward the elevator.

After entering, I had to show two fingers to an overhead camera to denote the floor where I was meeting William. He and I were escorted into a small room with a table and two chairs. Striking to me, because if I had interviewed him in state prison just a few days earlier, he most likely would have been in shackles and/or a cage, like the inmates I had spoken to at three state prisons a few months previously.

William knew I was an expert for his release team, but his warmth and respect in greeting me seemed an integral aspect of who he now was as a person rather than a false front to impress me. A barrel-chested, muscular man, he limped in on a cane, as if his powers had been sapped away by so many years in prison.

His life was full of tragedies from the start, not atypical of three-strikes lifers.

William's parents never married and, although his mother was a nurse, his father was an illiterate alcoholic. His dad was physically abusive to him and his mother. He shared an early traumatic memory of his father beating his mother on her head. When his father broke a glass fixture over William's crib, she struck back by cutting at her husband's throat.

He left the family after that incident, but William explained how his father kidnapped him a few years later, and how very frightening this was to him. He continues to this day to have disturbing dreams of his father beating his mother, stepmother, sisters, brothers and himself.

A few years later, his father was granted more court-approved time with William.

His memories of these years include his father forcing him to wear a hanger around his head and purposely keeping him awake all night. When William was ten, his father married a woman who had two sons. These boys were seven and eight years older than he was. William painfully recalls that they both performed aggressive sexual acts on him, as well as beat him. The abuse didn't stop until the older boys were both institutionalized at Boy's Ranch. He also tearfully shared that he'd had consensual sex at the age of 13 with his 27-year-old stepmother.

It is not surprising in this familial environment that William began smoking marijuana at age ten. He also set two fires and had trouble with schoolwork. He beat up a bully who repeatedly provoked him when he was 11. He also had brief counseling at this age for aggressive behavior toward a female peer.

His mom worked all the time, leaving him a latch-key kid. Even in his mother's house, he was subjected to repeated beatings from his stepfather. His stepfather also had sex with William's older sister, who was on long-term psychiatric disability. William told me his sister offered to have sex with him, but he informed me proudly that he turned her down.

William's maternal grandmother was diagnosed with paranoid schizophrenia, and there is as well a strong history of criminal behavior in male relatives on both sides of his family. William's maternal grandmother was diagnosed with paranoid schizophrenia, and there is as well a strong history of criminal behavior in male relatives on both sides of his family.

William attended five different high schools where he did poorly academically, but excelled in sports until he dropped out his senior year. While in high school he was a regular user of marijuana and cocaine, often stealing to support his habit. Consequently, he was convicted of grand theft and served two six-month sentences in juvenile facilities.

In 1986, at the age of 18, he earned his first strike for robbery and residential burglary, and spent three years in prison for a theft related to his cocaine addiction. William was convicted for nonviolent drug-related offenses in 1987 and 1990. Involved with Palo Alto gangs from a very early age, he managed to extricate himself from gang life in 1990, though he remained dependent on cocaine. He made his first suicide attempt around this time, in reaction to the murder of his nephew.

William was arrested in 1992 for battery with serious injury committed while he was in the San Mateo county jail. This incident was his response to a fellow inmate who made a racial slur about the verdict in the Rodney King trial. Offenses like this, committed in the violence-prone climate of custody, are often causes of a second or third strike.

William was released to parole on March 23, 1994, and received a mental-health evaluation on April 4, 1994, by Dr. Phil Wilson, a psychiatrist. Dr. Wilson's well-documented diagnosis was posttraumatic stress disorder with a possible antisocial personality. Dr. Wilson noted his potential for violence at that time and continued him on Mellaril. A psychologist's evaluation done in May of 1994 cited William's IQ as 69, which was likely on the low side of his true level of functioning and in contrast to his actual achievement tests, which showed him functioning at an average level in basic academic skills.

In his clinical interview with me, he demonstrated good skills in focus, concentration, comprehension, memory, judgment, and abstract reasoning. He denied any hallucinations for several decades. A psychiatric evaluation by Dr. Douglas Harper dated Aug. 13, 1996, diagnosed only situational depression. He has also been on and off numerous antidepressant and antianxiety medications during his prison stays, which provided some relief from his depression and anxiety. He has been prescribed pain meds like codeine and tramadol, both of which can be addicting. His diagnosis in CDCR has consistently been "depression, not otherwise specified." This diagnosis, all too frequent in corrections, has been barred since fall of 2015, when the Diagnostic and Statistical Manual of Mental Disorders (DSM-5) was officially recognized.

Under the three-strikes law, William was sentenced on December 1, 1997, to 28 years to life for the nonviolent offenses of cloning cell phones and driving a stolen rental car. He said he borrowed the car from a friend and did not know it was stolen. He suffered a serious loss in 1999, when his live-in girlfriend of three years broke up with him because he wouldn't marry her. He made his last suicide attempt shortly after the breakup, when the enormity of this loss hit him. His hopes to reconcile with her were further dashed by his most recent offense.

William was devastated by his mother's death in 2004 and sobbed heavily during my interview when he spoke about her. He also cried when he described how his godmother had taken his mother's place and truly been there for him. His mother had left him $10,000. He claimed the guards told other inmates about his inheritance, and his peers bullied him for months to buy them things and pay protection.

During his sixteen years of incarceration for this offense, he committed five serious rules violations. Three of the five were in level IV institutions where the majority of inmate violence was racially related. As an example of the violence of prison culture, in 2006 fourteen male inmates died in CDCR as a result of assault/battery. In February 1999, William was stabbed. In November of the same year, in a climate of racial violence at Centinella State Prison, William participated in a fight between five African-Americans and two Caucasians. He was observed exchanging punches with a white inmate and lost 90 days' credit for this altercation.

William was transferred to High Desert State Prison on February 2, 2000. In 2002, almost 25 percent of inmate deaths due to assault in all of CDCR occurred at this facility. On July 28, 2007, William was observed in a fistfight with another inmate at the same time as a riot was occurring in another yard. He again lost 90 days' credit. Starting in 2007, he spent six years in facilities where inmate violence is common and demonstrated sufficient self-control not to fight or lose his temper. He claimed all his fights in custody were self-defense and took place years ago. It appeared to me his anger had burned out a few years before I met him.

He lost 30 days for possession of a cell phone on October 2008. Then, in April 2010, he lost 120 days for possession of marijuana. In 2011 he stole paper and envelopes from the chapel at Pelican Bay State Prison.

He reported to me that he felt caught in the middle during a summer 2013 hunger strike. He said he was coerced to skip meals by prison gang threats of violence and threatened by custodial intimations of being placed in punitive segregation if he did stop eating. He managed to take a middle ground, which left him unscathed by either party, perhaps demonstrating that he had learned to survive personal threats without recourse to violence in this often-combative setting.

William had sufficient physical and sexual abuse in his early years to be diagnosed with posttraumatic stress disorder. He still meets the criteria for that diagnosis. Individuals with PTSD, like William, are often quite vulnerable to physical threats.

I suspect that his early physical trauma led him to react in a protective way whenever there was a situation where he felt he would be made into a "punk." "Punk" is a term used in prisons to connote anal rape but can be generalized to any form of victimization.

He had in the past responded with physical force to such challenges, particularly in the climate of extreme brutality existing in most of the prisons where he has been housed.

For instance, in Pelican Bay, where he spent a great deal of time, mentally ill inmates—William's classification—constitute 15 percent of the population. Yet in 2012, 49 percent of custodial use of force was directed at mental-health inmates.

According to Steve Martin, CDCR's own expert on use of force in Coleman v. Brown, Pelican Bay had more fatal shootings than the combined total of all American prisons during one time period in the 1990s. William shared with me that the violent climate at High Desert State Prison in California is so explosive he much prefers the infamous Pelican Bay. He claimed he and many other inmates committed infractions to avoid a transfer to High Desert. His description of the chaos there was validated by a state investigation, reported by the *L.A. Times* on December 17, 2015. The investigators said there was an "entrenched culture of racism and violence" in which guards set inmates up for attack. Interesting, but not surprising. The Sacramento Bee reported a few days later that the correction officers' union filed a suit against the state prisons for agreeing with the inspector general's allegedly unsubstantiated attacks.

Recently, however, William appears to have overcome his early traumas. Together with new coping strategies, he no longer reacts to these types of threats with violence.

William has had several severe medical problems, some of which have been questioned as a way to manipulate the system for personal gain. The most severe physical issue has been a lower back problem, which led to the twisted back, sciatic pain and use of a cane that I observed. In the past, his back issues had led to a total inability to walk. Finally, in March of 2012, an MRI proved he had a basis for his back issues, including several protruding lumbar discs, spinal stenosis, spinal arthritis and scoliosis. His back condition is a progressive one and could require extensive medical care in the future, including one or more surgeries. He is currently unable to lift more than 25 pounds. He also has severe pain in both of his shoulders, high blood pressure, asthma and a strong family history of diabetes. His multiple severe medical problems are typical of the rapidly increasing number of older inmates in contemporary prisons.

William described himself as dedicated to his educational, vocational, and spiritual development while incarcerated. His records show that from 1998 to 2009 he received many reports describing him as a "diligent student" and a "conscientious worker." He received his GED in 2008 while incarcerated. From 2007 to 2011 he completed several courses with Set Free Prison Ministries and the Crossroad Bible Institute. Anticipating release, William had in place a viable program plan that included housing at a Christian home, called In The Name of the Loving Father, and a job offer at Retraining The Village in Belmont, California.

The job would be house manager, serving the homeless and helping with Bible studies. William also desired to resume his step work in Alcoholics Anonymous and, ultimately, to become a substance abuse counselor.

Shortly after the conclusion of his hearing, William was released from incarceration in order to begin his carefully planned new life of helping other disadvantaged people. William's case is an example of how revisions in the three-strikes law can be effective in releasing prisoners who have already served long prison sentences for a third nonviolent crime. His legal aid attorney's valiant efforts made his release possible by establishing a full after-care program and obtaining the funding for required expert witnesses. William's case is an example of how using a sentencing reform could contribute greatly to lessening overcrowding in California prisons, without indiscriminate release of potentially dangerous offenders. Three-strikes reforms are a result of the new national flexibility in sentencing procedures, a response to the draconian sentencing of the '90s, which filled our jails and prisons beyond capacity.

One-third of nine thousand prisoners sentenced under three strikes were considered sufficiently safe to be eligible for consideration of release under Prop 36. Six thousand were too unsafe to even be considered. As of February 2015, 2,008 inmates had been released under this program. Only one hundred thirty-two of those eligible were denied. Seven hundred similarly sentenced inmates lingered in California prisons without access to attorneys or courts that might have facilitated their release.

Of those who had been freed more than 18 months, only 4.7 percent had committed new crimes, compared to the average of about 45 percent in 18 months for most released felons. According to Stanford Law School's Justice Advocacy Project, if all eligible inmates were released, the state would save almost a billion dollars in ten years. However, like all prison-release projects, it is essential that inmates have prearranged housing, medical and psychiatric care, employment or training, and adequate starter funding for all these necessary modalities—or three-strikes release programs will be just another failed reform.

CHAPTER 9

My View of the 2013 California Prison Hunger Strike

———◆———

MANY OF THE PROBLEMS I encountered during my 2013 evaluation of CDCR helped me understand how the overall conditions led to the massive hunger strike that began on July 8, 2013, when 30,000 inmates refused meals and 2,300 skipped work or classes and threatened to continue to do so until their demands were met. The inmates' issues included wanting a five-year limit on solitary confinement, as well as education, rehabilitation and monthly phone calls while in the Secure Housing Unit (SHU).

The focus of my February 2013 visit was exclusively on mentally ill inmates as part of the Coleman suit, in which I first participated as an expert in 1992. The percentage of Coleman class (designated by CDCR as mentally ill) inmates had more than doubled over the twenty-year period, and their representation in the

SHU and the administrative segregation areas (Ad Seg is a slightly less deprived environment than SHU) skyrocketed to over 80 percent in some state prisons. In both the SHU and Ad Seg there is limited if any access to therapeutic, vocational and recreational services, with prolonged cell confinement and little human contact. Vast numbers of mentally inmates are in segregation for two main reasons:

Lack of coping skills to adapt to prison life and regulations

Correctional staff's lack of understanding of the role mental illness plays in their aberrant behavior.

There are reasons gang members and leaders need to be separated from other inmates, but all too many other prisoners, particularly those who are mentally ill, get swept up by custodial concerns and are placed in these segregated units for years. In segregation, the conditions of deprivation are so severe that mentally ill inmates are much more vulnerable to suicide and psychotic breakdowns than they would be in less secure and isolated areas of the prison, yet they are placed in segregation specifically because of their psychological problems.

In March 2012, CDCR issued a position statement on dealing with the gang problem in its prisons, choosing to define inmates known to be a part of a gang or suspected of being in one as a Security Threat

Group [STG]. There appear to be as many acronyms in the correctional system as there are problems.

In this position paper, partially motivated by a much smaller hunger strike in 2011, CDCR recognized "a need to evaluate current strategies and implement new approaches to address evolving gang trends." The organization accepted that its current approach was "initially adopted more than 25 years ago." The position statement advocated a strategy of graduated housing, programs and privileges based on positive behavior, with consequences for continued gang behavior. This is a valid theoretical approach, but untenable in the way it was implemented.

Corrections determined that an essential element for this method to succeed would be "the continuing evolution of our existing intelligence network." This approach is fraught with difficulties to whatever extent it involves inmate informants. The slightest rumor of an inmate snitching or even an early release from SHU invariably increases suspicion of *ratting*, and can lead to a severe beating or even death. This part of inmate culture is very difficult to change. If the informant survives the beating, he will be placed back in a segregated housing unit for his own protection for the duration of his stay at his current or any other penal institution (news of a snitch travels fast and far).

The most feared gangs are Aryan Brotherhood, Black Guerilla Family, Mexican Mafia, Nazi Low Riders, Northern Structure, Nuestra Familia, and Texas Syndicate.

Secondary STGs include Crips, Nortenos, Bloods, Surenos and White Supremacist, which are often subservient to the first group of gangs.

It was a stunning revelation to me that four inmates housed in the highly isolated and secure SHU of Pelican Bay State Prison were able to organize the 2013 hunger strike. But that is the culture and structure of prisons, and the authority exerted by these isolated men is one reason these inmates are segregated. Two of these organizers were leaders of the Mexican Mafia and Nuestra Familia, one a member of the Black Gorilla Family, and the fourth likely a leader of the Aryan Brotherhood. They were housed near each other so they could be more easily controlled, but that strategy backfired and drew them together into an influential group called The Short Corridor Collective.

The step-down procedure necessary to leave the SHU, put into effect well before the hunger strike, is a Sisyphean task that requires a minimum of four years of untarnished behavior. Each progression is based upon intelligence and the absence of confirmed gang behaviors, and requires specifically designed units for the step-downs.

Several committees for placement then evaluate the inmate after four years of good behavior. If approved for transition from a SHU, the prisoner would spend his fifth year in a transitional housing program called a Special Needs Yard (SNY). However, there was such a desperate shortage of SNY housing during my assessment that a new category, Lack of Bed (LOB), was created for inmates waiting in segregation for placement. In fact, I saw no specialized facilities to handle step-downs during my visits to three prisons. However, nearly half of the first 400 inmates reviewed were reportedly released to the general population.

The irony of the hunger strike is that although most of the strikers' demands were for removal of conditions that were cruel and inhumane, the strike was organized by four of CDCR's most dangerous and isolated gang leaders, and confirms how powerful a coalition of prison gangs can be even if the leaders are separated from all other inmates. In 2012, the Short Corridor Collective attempted to shift alliances and issued an "agreement to end hostilities between racial groups" and instead focus against "corrections, informants, snitches, rats, and obstructionists."

This hunger strike was by far the largest protest in California prison history. Four days after the strike began 29,000 inmates were still refusing food. However, the numbers began to drop sharply as inmates reported threats to search their cells, seize their food stashes, force-feed them and place them in solitary confinement. William, profiled in the previous chapter, had been housed in a high-level security institution at the beginning of the strike. He said he felt pulled apart between prison gangs threatening violence if he ate and custody threatening him with the SHU or force-feeding if he didn't eat. He managed to survive being caught between the two forces, and was even able to refuse corrections' tempting offers of pizza and buffalo wings early in the strike.

I also spoke with another former inmate who was at the California Men's Colony during the hunger strike. He reported that all the inmates at CMC knew about the strike a week before it began. They bought all the commissary food in advance they could afford and simply ate that instead of the food in the dining room. He said he and all the other inmates there were restricted to their bunks as punishment for not eating. He actually liked the dining room food and, despite his commissary stash, lost ten pounds during the strike.

At Pelican Bay, protesting inmates complained that blasts of cold air were used to further weaken them. By July 26, 630 inmates were still refusing food and 18 had medical complications. On July 27 the number fasting was 601. An inmate in segregation—who may originally have participated in the strike and later withdrew from it—hanged himself. Other inmates stated he had tried to get medical help before his death. Three hundred sixty-one inmates were still on strike on August 1, and the possibility of force-feeding was becoming more and more likely, though stirring quite a controversy as to whether the procedure is inherently inhumane.

On August 16, former state senator Tom Hayden reported that at least 300 inmates were still fasting. He suggested implementation of "conflict-resolution measures" rather than compliance with Gov. Jerry Brown's demand to end the fast before any issues could be resolved. Also on August 16, NBCnews.com reported that dozens of inmates had been sent to hospitals or prison infirmaries. According to the media report, however, the number of inmates who had not eaten was down to 118.

In my assessment of three California prisons the February before the hunger strike—Corcoran State Prison, California Institution for Men in Chino (CIM) and Central California Prison for Women in Chowchilla—I was alarmed by the extensive use of SHU and Ad Seg for the mentally ill, often for reasons wholly unrelated to disciplinary infractions. At every institution I toured, I met individuals on the mental-health caseload who were housed in segregation due to a shortage of appropriate beds. These individuals experienced long periods of severe idleness, lack of human contact, and extreme confinement, all to the worsening of their mental health. Most were not gang members, yet they were being subjected to the same conditions gang members faced—conditions that led to the hunger strike.

The situation that concerned me most was at CIM, where I encountered widespread use of Administrative Segregation Units (ASUs) for mentally ill patients with no apparent disciplinary infractions. Even the state's experts agreed that many of these individuals were "housed in an Administrative Segregation Unit for their own protection; not because they posed a danger to others." CIM had classified many of these individuals as "LOB"—"lack of bed." The vast majority of the inmates in the Cypress Hall administrative segregation housing unit at CIM were LOBs, not inmates who had been designated for administrative segregation.

Unlike inmates who are formally placed in administrative segregation, these individuals had undergone no due process and, in many cases, received no explanation before being placed in isolation. They had no sense of when their confinement in the ASU would end, and their requests for information about their future often went unanswered.

Another example of the inhumanity of segregation is the extremely high suicide rate in these units in California prisons. Only 5.8 percent of the overall prison population is housed in Ad Seg yet in 2012, 34 percent of suicides occurred there. The Special Master assigned to monitor CDCR found this difference "staggering."

On July 25, 2013, the Short Corridor Group issued a statement typical of inmates' response to oppressive measures: "The attempted repression of our protest has not broken our spirits. In fact it has only helped to strengthen each of us—individually and collectively."

My colleague and fellow Coleman expert Dr. Craig Haney wrote in *Reforming Punishment* that inmates join gangs to band together to protect themselves from the dangers of imprisonment. They "align with a group in order to achieve an internal sense of psychological security . . . The gang produces order in a world of disorder . . . a stable identity and a sense of security." Haney notes that, in the end, if the inmate is "identified as a gang member [that] virtually always results in a worsened rather than improved quality of prison life." The gang member is placed in the harsh conditions of punitive isolation where "alienation, anger, and conflict tend to feed and reinforce gang membership. The lack of programming or other meaningful activities forces them even more intensely on gang-related activities."

A former high-ranking California prison official confided to me that corrections has an investment in keeping the gang system alive. He shared confidentially that in his opinion CDCR needs the gangs to continue because they split the prison population into smaller groups, making them easier to control than if they were more united.

Dr. Haney's solution to the gang problem is to provide meaningful and genuine work and activity, individual counseling, and bridges to community-based organizations. The goal is to create "transitional pathways" to meaningful activities that can overcome the social devastation of prisons and, even more so, of solitary confinement.

In March of 2013, 734 inmates were defined as Coleman class, i.e., mentally ill, and housed in SHUs in California prisons. The damage to these individuals from living in an SHU is so profound they should never be housed in this type of solitary confinement. In general they are not capable of organizing a protest against their dehumanized conditions, but I hope the hunger strike will have cast light on their plight in the SHU as well as that of alleged gang members.

The policy makers of the state of California finally agreed at the end of August 2013 to hold public hearings on conditions in maximum-security prisons, vowing that these hearings would result in proposals for policy changes. By then, nearly ten fasting inmates a day collapsed or required serious medical care. After being apprised of the legislative hearings, the leaders of the protest were permitted to communicate directly with one another and agreed to call off the strike as of September 5, 2013. This concluded what was arguably the largest peaceful prison protest in US history.

Over the following two years, 1,100 inmates were slowly released from solitary. In September 2015, the *L.A. Times* reported that CDCR agreed to release 1,800 more of the 6,400 inmates still housed in solitary confinement. I agree with my fellow Coleman expert, psychiatrist Terry Kupers, who said, "This is a game changer."

However, the full process of release was expected to take two more years, and 4,600 of these inmates would remain in the psychologically dangerous environment of solitary. Corrections moves slowly and with great caution, and I understand the need to do so. The state prison guards union opposed the settlement out of fear of a return to the violence of the '80s. Mutual paranoia between inmates and officers has built up for decades, and the vast numbers of mentally ill have further overwhelmed the system. Corrections doesn't know where to put psychiatric inmates because they don't fit anywhere in the state prison system as it presently exists.

The 2013 hunger strike certainly brought the deplorable conditions of solitary confinement to public awareness. This is an example of the ability of inmates to be one of many agents of change in this complicated system. The diminished use of solitary as of Fall 2015 led me to believe that this hunger strike helped bring about meaningful changes in California's overcrowded prison system. Only time will tell if the changes will progress or if the omnipresent pendulum will swing back to punitive approaches once again.

Solutions

CHAPTER 10

The Judge Gets the Final Word

———◆———

JUDGE KARLTON PASSED AWAY ON July 11, 2015, of slowly progressive heart disease.

Fortunately, he released his final decree 15 months before he died. I will again take the liberty of translating his legalese and mental-health terminology into everyday language. My personal opinions are in italics.

    A. The judge's rulings on housing the mentally ill in the sensory and socially depriving environment of segregation were:

        1. Prohibit any mentally ill inmate from being placed in existing administrative segregation units [Ad Seg] when clinicians determine there is substantial risk of worsening of mental illness, total mental breakdown, or suicide from such placement. *If enforced,*

*and if mental health staff assert themselves,
this could substantially limit the housing of
the mentally ill in solitary. But in the present
system and architecture, what—if any—appropriate housing exists for them?*

2. Defendants shall provide monthly reports
   to the court and the Special Master on
   whether mental-health intensive treatment
   units meet standards for adequate care.

   *The Special Master was appointed in 1995
   to ensure that judicial orders for improvement
   of medical care, mental-health treatment and
   overcrowding were followed. The master selected a team of psychiatric experts to assess
   compliance.*

   *I was informed that corrections vetoed me
   as a member of this team because they felt I was
   biased against them, which undoubtedly I was
   at that time. The Master and his excellent staff
   have been monitoring and reporting on CDCR's
   lack of compliance since 1995, yet continuous legal
   suits have been necessary to move toward safe and
   constitutional treatment. As previously described,
   these units are woefully inadequate physically and
   also desperately understaffed. How can requirements ever be met under these conditions without
   total renovation and reeducation?*

3. Defendants shall not admit any psychiatric patient at the EOP level [the most severe mentally ill] to any Ad Seg unit that does not meet these requirements for two consecutive months.

> *Corrections have been known to move an inmate out and back again or to a different location and start the count of days spent in segregation over from day one. This practice must be monitored and prevented.*

4. Defendants shall file a revised policy concerning strip searches in EOP ASU hubs.

> *Can they individualize strip searches to only inmates who are security risks, or is there too much fear of all prisoners, including or particularly the mentally ill? How many times can guards be stabbed by makeshift weapons wielded by the minority of inmates and not mistrust and fear harm from all inmates?*

5. Defendants are prohibited from housing any psychiatrically ill inmate in any SHU (secure housing unit or most severe solitary confinement) in California unless that inmate's treating clinician certifies that (a) the behavior leading to the SHU assignment was not the product of mental illness and the inmate's illness did not prevent

him from conforming his conduct to institutional requirements, (b) the inmate's
mental illness can be safely and adequately
managed in the SHU for the entire length
of the SHU term, and (c) the inmate does
not face a substantial risk of worsening of
his or her mental illness as a result of confinement in a SHU. In addition, defendants
are prohibited from returning any seriously
mentally ill inmate to any SHU unit if the
inmate has at any time following placement
in a SHU required a higher level of mental-
health care.

*I can't imagine how an inmate's mental ill-
ness can ever be managed in a SHU for an extended stay. If [c] were enforced, this would end
the vicious cycle of "psych and return," where
an inmate has a remission of psychiatric illness
in a mental-health bed, then repeatedly breaks
down in the SHU. Implementation will require
much greater respect for the opinions of clinicians than has existed for decades.*

B. Judge Karlton's ruling about the use of force
and disciplinary measures was:

1. Defendants shall work under the guidance
of the Special Master to revise their use of

force policies and procedures as required by this order.

2. The Special Master shall report to the court within six months whether defendants have adequately implemented the RVR [*rule violation report*] policies and procedures agreed to in 2011.

    Despite adopting reasonable policies and procedures in the past four years, CDCR had not successfully implemented them. Can they be trusted now to correct inadequacies in the disciplinary process for the mentally ill?

3. With respect to the use of force, the court specifically held that the defendants' recent revisions to their procedures concerning the use of force represented cruel and unusual punishment. This is because, among other things, the revised policies do not require consideration of an inmate's ability to conform his or her conduct to the directive or rule in question and do not give mental-health clinicians enough authority over decisions regarding use of force.

    If done properly, corrections would have to give mental-health staff power they are inherently reluctant to give in any penal setting, and mental-health staff would have to do thorough examinations and stand by them.

4. The court also required the defendants to develop additional guidance regarding the use of the potentially harmful expandable baton. The defendants were ordered to make additional revisions to their policies within sixty days, and the Special Master was to oversee the process.

   I agree these batons were abused on mentally ill inmates at times, but taking an officer's weapons away can be quite threatening to him/her.

5. The order specifically says inmates' attorneys will have input into the development of the new policies, and they plan to participate as actively in this process as they are permitted.

6. Modification of the use of "management status" [previously described as depriving inmates of most of their privileges without due process] so this practice can be reviewed by the Special Master as part of his review of the implementation of defendants' RVR policies and procedures.

C. The judge ruled on housing the undisciplined mentally ill with inmates who are being disciplined as follows:

1. Within thirty days from the date of this order defendants shall file a plan to limit or eliminate altogether placement of class members [all mentally ill inmates] removed from the general population for nondisciplinary reasons in any administrative segregation unit that houses disciplinary segregation inmates.

2. Sixty days from the date of this order, defendants will be prohibited from placing any class members removed from the general population for nondisciplinary reasons for more than seventy-two hours in administrative segregation units.

   These two provisions eliminate the Lack of Bed [LOB] category and the option of placing mentally ill in segregation except in emergency situations. However, since many symptoms of mental illness are considered worthy of discipline by CDCR, this modifier could be used to avoid changing present practices.

3. Defendants shall work under the guidance of the Special Master to develop a protocol for administrative segregation decisions, including a plan for alternative housing that will prevent placement of any Coleman class member in existing Ad Seg units when

clinical information shows substantial risk of mental breakdown or suicide from this placement.

D. Suicide Prevention Measures

The court emphasized a previous ruling that for seriously mentally ill inmates, placement in California's segregated housing units, including both Ad Seg units and SHUs, can and does cause serious psychological harm.

Judge Karlton did not grant a blanket exclusion of the mentally ill from segregation. Instead, defendants will be prohibited from housing any seriously mentally ill inmate at any SHU in California unless that inmate's behavior is not a result of mental illness. The ruling also limits time in Ad Seg to only three days for emergencies.

This ruling will depend for its effectiveness on the competence and assertiveness of mental-health staff as well as the willingness of correctional staff to utilize their recommendations. As I have previously described, CDCR has managed to not fully comply with many earlier rulings related to overcrowding and/or unconstitutional treatment of the mentally ill for more than two decades.

CDCR initially responded to Judge Karlton's rulings by issuing new policies for complying with the court order for housing the mentally ill in segregation and for use of force. Corrections' plan for these disturbed inmates in segregation made no provision to release or exclude them from these conditions when their illness puts them at risk for mental breakdown or suicide.

Also, CDCR planned to develop an alternative segregation program for the mentally ill, but without the essential therapeutic components to enable meaningful treatment or suicide prevention. In its initial response, corrections did not provide for measures to prevent the cycle of returning inmates to the conditions that caused them to be psychotic or suicidal after prison psychiatric treatment. Nor did CDCR provide for adequate consideration of mental-health recommendations in the behavior leading to an assignment in solitary.

On August 1, 2014, CDCR issued further revised policies that it claimed reflected "a systemwide practice and culture change in the ways correctional staff will relate to the mentally ill." These changes provided for a mental-health provider to evaluate the "totality of circumstances involved" before force is used on a mentally ill inmate. CDCR proposes a cool-down period during which a mental-health provider will attempt to defuse the situation. I have described brief, unsuccessful interventions in previous chapters. What will change the prison culture so there are therapeutic, not punitive, interactions between inmates and staff, regardless whether they are corrections officers or mental-health workers?

Eventually, corrections agreed to all of Judge Karlton's conditions, which *The New York Times* described as "sweeping" in an August 3, 2014, article. In its response, CDCR stated it planned to "limit or eliminate Coleman class (i.e., mentally ill) members removed from the general population for nondisciplinary reasons from Ad Seg units that house inmates for disciplinary reasons," amend use of force and body search policy, limit use of management cells, and enhance treatment for the most disturbed of the mentally ill.

Corrections also agreed to consider "the role of mental illness in an inmate's ability to comply with staff directives," utilize mental-health input before use of force, and consider "when, if ever, those judgments may be overridden by custody staff."

The department pledged that by the end of 2014 it would complete "extensive revisions to the expandable baton, firearms, chemical agents and general use-of-force lesson plans," and that training would begin by February 2015. Officers would be trained to recognize and understand mental illness, collaborate with mental-health staff, and exhaust every reasonable alternative to force. Custody would not override mental-health recommendations against use of force and/or pepper spray unless senior management approved the override.

Thus senior custodial management could still have veto power over mental health recommendations in regard to use of force.

Judge Karlton also ruled in the related but less-publicized case of Hecker v. CDCR on August 6, 2014, that severe mentally ill prisoners would have access to jobs, educational and vocational programs, and earn good time (a shortened sentence for good behavior) for these activities. Also, accommodations would allow inmates on heat-sensitive meds [most antipsychotic meds cause increased sensitivity to heat] to have time out of their cell on warm days. The Americans with Disabilities Act (ADA) reinforces this ruling.

Even the skeptical inmates' attorneys considered these responses to Karlton's orders remarkable progress. I agree strongly with inmate attorney Jeffrey Bornstein, who stated the proposal is "a great first step" but "the devil is in the training" and the ability of corrections to make substantial changes in its prison culture. Michael Bien, who has been a lead attorney in the Coleman case for over twenty years, said CDCR's response represented "meaningful reforms that go a long way." Not only will the Special Master monitor these changes, but so too will several teams of inmates' attorneys, including Bornstein and Bien.

Much of the credit for these recent achievements goes to Judge Karlton, who was at the cusp of retirement at age 79 when he gave his ruling, and who had tried to resolve these difficult issues for years. He retired on September 26, 2014, to a standing ovation from other judges and friends, who described him as a man of passion on the bench.

Judge Lawrence K. Karlton passed away nine months after he retired. He was known for his legal opinions benefiting individuals who needed help, such as mentally ill inmates and undocumented immigrants. He had suffered from a heart valve problem for several years, which included the trials and rulings described in the preceding chapters. His awareness of his illness was undoubtedly one reason he had expressed to me his doubts about writing his final opinion on the case.

Judge Karlton's death left me feeling quite sad. I had felt like we were two white-bearded old friends chatting about an important but difficult problem for which we were both passionately trying to find a workable solution.

In March 2015, US District Judge Thelton Henderson ruled for a gradual lifting of federal monitoring of medical and mental-health care at CDCR, having determined there had been substantial improvement in these services. He did emphasize that each of the state's 34 prisons must pass an inspection before returning to state control. However, Inspector General Robert A. Barton of CDCR was designated to perform these inspections. I wondered how impartial that office would be.

In July 2015, Folsom State Prison became the first state facility to regain control over inmate health care from the federal receiver. By the end of 2015, Folsom was the only one of the 34 prisons whose medical care had been returned to state control. It appears this office is acting more fairly than I had anticipated. I will continue to watch with interest CDCR's ability to make meaningful changes in the deeply entrenched culture of how all inmates are handled, let alone those who are mentally ill.

The shift toward easing prison conditions and monitoring changes is not limited to California. In December 2015 the New York State prison system settled a suit brought by the New York Civil Liberties Union to fundamentally reform the harsh conditions and lengthy stays in isolation by agreeing to two years of performance monitoring. In a January 4, 2016, op-ed piece by Michelle Deitch, *The New York Times* called for implementation of an independent government monitoring body for all New York prisons and jails. This recommendation reflects the American Bar Association's national policy on oversight of jails and prisons. Civil liberties attorneys in many other states have implemented suits to provide constitutionally mandated mental health care to prisoners. In a trial, which began in the state of Alabama in December 2016, my fellow Coleman expert Craig Haney described some of the worst conditions for treatment of the mentally ill he'd ever seen in any prison.

CHAPTER 11

New Takes on Proven Treatment Approaches

I CURRENTLY WORK WITH TWO treatment programs that seem very different on the surface. Both, however, provide treatment for severe mental illness, drug and alcohol abuse and addiction, and an alternative to incarceration. They are Northbound Treatment Services in Costa Mesa, California, and The Friendship Shelter in Laguna Beach, California.

Northbound is a comprehensive treatment program providing a full range of care to addicts and alcoholics, many of whom also have mental illness and/or are in the program as an alternative to incarceration. Its location near the beach, reputation, and outreach attract clients from all social classes and areas of the United States.

The program starts with medically supervised detoxification and stabilization, followed by a system with various levels and a wide variety of treatment approaches. Each phase builds upon the other and addresses every aspect of a person's life, with biological, social, spiritual, recreational, and psychological interventions to support entry into early recovery.

Northbound greatly values the philosophy and Twelve Steps of Alcoholics Anonymous (AA) as an integral part of recovery. Clients are strongly encouraged to attend meetings, work the steps, obtain a sponsor, and receive the fellowship and comprehensive support offered by AA. Not all clients commit to AA, but those who do are more likely to lead happy, sober lives. Northbound recently added a Refuge Recovery group, with an emphasis on spirituality, meditation, and a Buddhist-oriented twelve steps.

The medical philosophy of Northbound is that no addicting or abusable medications are used to treat concomitant mental illness once detoxification is complete. However, addicts and alcoholics are known to abuse many medications, some of which the vast majority of patients and their doctors wouldn't dream could be mind-altering, like the antidepressant Welbutrin or the anti-seizure drug Neurontin or Cogentin, a medicine used to treat Parkinson's Disease. These types of medications are prescribed when necessary and are rarely abused in the program. All patients with co-occurring mental illness are placed in an intensive treatment program addressing their specific needs for both mental-health and drug-abuse treatment services.

The core program at Northbound has four phases, with increasing privileges at each stage. Seven residences total 101 beds, which are often filled close to capacity, as are over 50 outpatient slots. Each client receives a full psychiatric and psychosocial assessment, and therapy is individually tailored to the whole person. Everyone is assigned a therapist for intensive psychotherapy as well as a case manager. There is a therapist who addresses issues of trauma utilizing EMDR and CBT. Most case managers have solid recovery from addictions as do most house managers and drivers. The majority of the therapists are degreed professionals who are not in recovery. All residents attend at least four therapy groups and a twelve-step meeting daily.

Alongside the intensive therapy is a strong emphasis on teaching residents to have sober fun. In this vein there is beach time with optional surfing and stand-up paddle boarding, gym participation, swimming, skiing, hiking, yoga, bungee jumping, kickboxing, bowling, equine therapy, laser tag, and a spirited music group led by a professional drummer with over 20 years of sobriety. There is even a color war like the days of summer camp and a piñata party.

A four-day intensive family program is a vital part of every resident's treatment. The families share and comfort the wounds of addiction in each other. They also learn effective communication, boundary setting, and how to support recovery without enabling.

A unique aspect of the treatment approach is the College and Career Bound Academy. Clients can enroll in any type of training or education program nearby. There are close affiliations with UC Irvine, several community colleges, fashion and culinary institutes, art and trade schools as well as many job opportunities. Performance in work and academic settings helps staff and clients evaluate if sobriety and personality changes can be sustained under the stress of dealing with work and other aspects of the world outside the protection of residential treatment.

Clients may also complete an on-site extensive course to obtain a drug and alcohol counseling certificate as part of the Academy. This provides a marketable skill for jobs as a technician or case manager in other rehab programs after six months of sobriety. Many then return to work at Northbound after a full year of sobriety.

Northbound continues the concept of long-term care and follow-up with The Bridge, which provides a gradual transition to the outside world, followed by an intensive outpatient program. There is even a further step-down, called Support, where there are case management, random drug and alcohol screening, and AA support. The overall description of the program makes it seem terribly expensive, but the cost for a year's treatment is about $50,000, the same as a year in a California state prison.

A typical day for me as medical director and addiction psychiatrist starts off at the detoxification program, simply called 180 because it is the beginning of a 180-degree turn in an addicted person's life.

A wide variety of patients awaits me each morning at this sprawling six-bedroom, one-story ranch home turned into a detox center. Rehabs and board and care homes are plentiful in this neighborhood, and their occupants often cycle by on beach cruisers as I approach the small, well-manicured front lawn of 180. One of our nurses greets me with a fresh cup of coffee, and the cook quickly tries to tempt me with steaming, home-baked carrot cake or banana pancakes. Everyone at 180 loves the cook, and why not? Nurturing meals prepared with care are an important part of alleviating the painful withdrawal from drugs and alcohol once we are able to relieve symptoms to the extent eating is a possibility.

The first patient I see is often a heroin and/or Oxycodone, Roxicodone, Vicodin opiate pill-dependent person in early withdrawal with a bit of methamphetamine, six milligrams or more of Xanax, a few joints of marijuana and/or a pint or two of alcohol mixed in.

He or she is most often also on a variety of psychiatric medications, one or two for each of several psychiatric diagnoses often made while their well-meaning psychiatrists were not aware they were still misusing drugs and alcohol. We see patients requiring withdrawal and stabilization from every drug imaginable, including Robitussin cough syrup, GHB, Adderall, Spice and bath salts.

Opiate withdrawal is the most painful of all, but not potentially life-threatening like withdrawal from sedatives and alcohol, where seizures or DTs can be deadly. It is not unusual to see an addict switch back and forth among many types of drugs depending on current symptoms, mood, price, or availability, so detoxification is often complicated. Detox usually takes five to seven days, but if a patient has been on a long-acting opiate like methadone or Suboxone for years, it can require several weeks.

Many of our clients have come from very successful families and attended fine colleges, but once addiction kicks in, they will do anything to support their habit, and then their behavior resembles that of hard-core street addicts. We commonly see misdemeanors and nonviolent felonies like petty theft, shoplifting, drug possession, or sales and prostitution committed by individuals who had previously led comfortable and promising lives.

Many were accomplished athletes who gave up their sport after a debilitating injury or argument with a coach or were promising students who pressed too hard. Their lives often began to fall apart after these early failures.

Chronic pain patients often have a slowly progressive addiction where they build up a tolerance and gradually need higher doses of opiates prescribed by their doctors.

Over time the opiates provide only relief from withdrawal symptoms and little or no alleviation of pain. Even chronic pain patients with no history of addiction can start to act like addicts, consulting multiple doctors and forging prescriptions. They are often shocked when their physical pain lessens or even disappears after detoxification is complete.

Every once in a while a pure alcoholic enters detox. It could be a homemaker who has hidden her two bottles of wine a day with a nap before the family comes home, a man who sees himself as a connoisseur of fine wine or alcohol, or even a guy who consumes "only" twelve to twenty-four cans of beer a day. Throw in a few Xanax or Klonopin a day and we have a potentially dangerous withdrawal with a risk of seizures or extreme mental confusion (delirium). Some heavy drinkers have so saturated every cell in their bodies with alcohol that after they complete the withdrawal process, they are unable to walk for days. More commonly, we see alcoholics who also abuse a wide variety of drugs as well as drink excessively.

After I finish treating the detox patients, I turn to those in 180 who have been referred directly after a month or two in a psychiatric hospital. Most of them are seriously mentally ill and/or suicidal. Several have drug-induced psychoses.

A typical patient of this type entered Northbound at the end of April 2015. Chris, as I will call her, was a direct transfer from a leading Midwestern psychiatric hospital. She presented as a petite 18-year-old with striking, neon-green hair. She was admitted to that hospital after she and her boyfriend both dropped acid and he tried to kill her. She'd had problems with marijuana, alcohol, and cocaine since the age of 13 and had used hallucinogens at least a dozen times. Several months before this incident, this same boyfriend asked her to choose between him leaving or strangling her. Chris chose strangling and fortunately survived. She was placed in a psychiatric hospital for six days at that time with a diagnosis of PTSD.

Chris was referred to Northbound for intensive treatment, not only for her personality and addiction issues but to fulfill a court requirement. She had become confused after a minor traffic accident and drove off to a nearby retail store. A zealous district attorney decided to prosecute her for leaving the scene of an accident, so she was ordered by the court to complete treatment or go to jail.

I am often amazed at the arbitrary and prejudicial nature of our judicial system.

So many individuals commit one nonviolent crime after another and, particularly if they come from privileged families, are given only minimal consequences. Others are punished severely for what amounts only to the consequences of poverty.

Chris was aware of how destructive her relationship with her boyfriend was, but continued to be drawn to him. She could see how her suffering in the relationship was connected to her propensity to self-inflict bruises on her legs, which she often did when she felt a need to punish herself. Surprisingly, given her abuse of self and drugs, she ate only organic vegan food.

She showed no signs of psychotic thinking and stated she was committed to sobriety at the time of her initial meeting with me.

Chris focused her in-depth psychotherapy on letting go of her relationship with her former boyfriend. After three months in the program, she felt she could close that chapter in her life. She completed the Fourth Step of AA, which consists of a "fearless moral inventory" of strengths and weaknesses, and was ready to share this with her outside sponsor. She entered the college-bound program, determined to become a therapist. Chris would undoubtedly have languished in a county jail were it not for her social class and health insurance.

Another group of clients of a different type are members or relations of a blue-collar union. Often these individuals have survived the wreckage of the ghetto through well-paying union jobs but maintain ties to the drug-infested world around them. Their gangbanger clothes and tattoos provide an interesting contrast to the college dropouts described above. Yet the drugs both groups abuse are quite similar.

Jimmy D is the son of a longshoreman who had stayed sober from alcohol for the past ten years. His mother was very active in her church. Jimmy D first entered Northbound in the summer of 2014. He was dressed in his typical outfit of baggy shorts belted below his waist and hanging below his knees, along with a loose football jersey and a Dodger's cap. He'd had multiple stints in local jails in the past. His body was covered with tattoos of skulls and knives.

When he arrived, he was hallucinating critical voices and had a detailed delusional system about a baby who never existed. He was overly concerned about this fictitious child and thought of nothing else. I determined that his psychosis was due to smoking large amounts of methamphetamine and placed him on gradually increasing doses of Seroquel, a powerful antipsychotic medication. When his psychosis continued despite high doses, a second major tranquilizer, Risperdal, was added. His hallucinations and delusions gradually resolved and totally cleared within six weeks.

Jimmy D continued in the program for another two months in order to learn sober coping skills, stabilize without psychotic symptoms, and intensify his twelve-step work. With his psychosis resolved, an endearing quality emerged, and he became very well-liked. His roly-poly body and endearing broad smile were irresistible. He left in mid-November, feeling quite happy, and espoused a commitment to sobriety. He was still on one antipsychotic medicine, but at a moderate dose to prevent a return to psychosis.

Jimmy stayed sober for several months, but he slipped away from AA and Narcotics Anonymous, stopped his meds, and hung out with his meth-using buddies. As soon as he used methamphetamine again, this time with heroin, he began to hear critical voices, but he still continued to use both drugs. He often repeated to himself, "Dr. K. told me I would damage my brain if I used meth again, and the voices would be worse." However, once the drugs took hold, nothing could stop him from using again and again. As soon as his family found out about his insanity, they set up a meeting with their union representative for health care, who quickly arranged for him to be readmitted.

When I saw him again in June of 2015, He was suffering from an even more severe methamphetamine psychosis than the first time I met him. He told me he was hearing the voices all the time and felt like his entire body was on fire. He was dazed, confused, and frightened, but he regretfully repeated his litany of, "Dr. K, Dr. K, you told me it would damage my brain, but I couldn't stop." His body shook with fear, tears poured down his still chubby cheeks, and he repeated, "I'm just so scared. My whole body hurts."

The constant voices were scaring him, telling him he might die. He was hallucinating large snakes and his most recent girlfriend. I immediately placed him on both the antipsychotic meds he did well on the last time I treated him. His recovery from psychosis was more tormented and took several weeks longer this time, but he again returned to a state free of psychotic symptoms.

In his psychotherapy, it was a struggle for him to give up his "thuggish" identity because it empowered him. We used his personal goal of being a "family man" to help him adopt new behaviors and rely on his personal warmth to build nurturing relationships with sober people who were not negative influences.

Jimmy left the program five months after he started his second stay, having completed all twelve steps, free of psychosis, and on one antipsychotic medication. He was also armed with tools to help him develop a strong sober identity so he could let go of feeling like a thug.

Despite my many years in this field, I am still amazed when a formerly high-achieving college student tells me their drugs of choice are IV heroin and methamphetamine. Of course, I also see the occasional student specialist in manufacturing or selling psychedelics coming to treatment after being suspended from the university or because he or she has prolonged, drug-induced psychosis. As a further reminder of blurring of drug choice and social class, Northbound recently admitted a longshoreman's self-educated son who knew more about making and using hallucinogenic drugs than any college student.

Northbound is expensive, but not more so than the costs of contemporary state prisons. The program demonstrates time and time again that former drug- and alcohol-abusing mentally ill "felons" can be turned around to a life where they do not recidivate but obtain jobs, albeit often in the recovery field, and bring money back to society. An independent academic research group studied the results of treatment at Northbound. The researchers found that this program showed 95 percent abstinence from alcohol and 97 percent from drugs one year after completion of treatment. In addition, there was substantial improvement in anxiety, depression and PTSD compared with when patients entered the program.

However, the follow-up study did not reach the majority of graduates, so the results are skewed in Northbound's favor.

The zero-tolerance policy of the above program is in sharp contrast to guidelines for the Friendship Shelter for the Homeless in Laguna Beach, where the philosophy is housing comes first, and abstinence will follow. The policy verges on a "no harm" philosophy of permissiveness.

This philosophy is the antithesis of my fifty years' experience in treating alcoholics and addicts, and a direct result of governmental funding priorities. But it has been interesting and challenging for me to work within this system where we evolve treatment plans but cannot insist that patients follow them as a condition of staying in these supportive programs.

The shelter has three programs offering a continuum of care but with differing standards for admission: the Alternative Sleep Location [ASL], the

Self-Sufficiency Program, and Permanent Supportive Housing.

The ASL is the only free, year-round emergency shelter program in the coastal area of Orange County, California. Forty-five of the most vulnerable homeless men and women in the region are sheltered here every night. Although there is some turnover, many of the clients from Laguna Beach return night after night. The program is open daily from 5 p.m. to 10 a.m. On an average night, six desperate homeless folks are turned away, some of whom sleep in the parking lot next to the ASL. The staff refers clients to many local agencies and helps them obtain health insurance through the Affordable Care Act.

Many of the homeless go on to the shelter's two longer-term programs.

The Self-Sufficiency Program provides housing, meals, and comprehensive support to 32 homeless men and women. Supportive services include case management; individual and group counseling; life skills training; on-site twelve-step groups; visual and dental care; job readiness and training; and access to a nurse, therapists and a psychiatrist. This is a 60-day program with a six- to eight-week waiting list. The extended wait for entry speaks to the desirability of the program as well as the paucity of such services in Orange County. Seventy-one percent of all clients who enter this program graduate successfully, having achieved sobriety, housing, and a sustainable income through a job or governmental stipend.

Residents of both the above programs may move on to scattered site Permanent Supportive Housing, where 60 formerly chronically homeless individuals are housed in apartments in several communities in South Orange County. Finding landlords willing to rent to homeless folks is difficult, but HUD funding makes it possible. These clients don't choose to be homeless. They suffer from debilitating medical and psychiatric illnesses. Housing is a critical beginning, but they also require a great deal of social support and help in navigating public social services and medical systems.

Without this program, they would be roaming the streets of Laguna Beach and surrounding communities, desperately seeking shelter and/or arrested and jailed. The daily costs at the Friendship Shelter range from $17 daily at the ASL to $65 for Permanent Supportive Housing. The latter is less than half the daily cost of incarceration.

Carl, a 29-year-old single man, is typical of the type of client residing in Supportive Housing who would otherwise be arrested frequently. He became unable to work at the age of 23 because of a severe bone disease for which he has required dozens of surgeries. He was always prescribed pain meds after his surgeries and was addicted and re-addicted time after time. When I first met him in March 2015 he was on Lyrica, in my opinion the best non-opiate reliever of chronic pain. He claimed he'd been sober for eight months but was still smoking marijuana. He contacted his sponsor via texts, but avoided twelve-step meetings.

Carl was referred for depression after his last surgery left him unable to walk without crutches—as he had been told it might. He had hoped to start a college program to become a medical technician, but didn't begin it because he was afraid to fail.

He had been arrested five times in his life and was incarcerated for 75 days when he didn't complete his court requirements. I agreed with the staff that he was depressed and prescribed the antidepressant Effexor because a different class of medication for depression had not worked for him in the past.

I saw Carl again a month later for a follow-up. Staff members told me they suspected he was using narcotics and denying it. He told me he had fallen ten days before and suffered a small fracture in his foot. He was given Norco (addicting hydrocodone) for the resulting pain and claimed he used five daily as prescribed and had stopped "cold turkey" five days before our meeting. His pupils were constricted, indicating recent narcotic use, which he denied. He missed two follow-up appointments with me, including one in September 2015, when I managed to speak with him on the phone. He came clean then because he knew he was in trouble. He was using a gram of heroin and more than 10 Norcos [hydrocodone] a day. He knew he couldn't stop on his own. He was taken to a local hospital where he was fully detoxified, placed on Suboxone maintenance, and given a fresh start.

Carl is typical of many homeless individuals who would be repeatedly incarcerated without the aid of an organization like the Friendship Shelter.

I have worked with patients from all levels of treatment at both Northbound and the Friendship Shelter. The majority are severely mentally ill and substance abusers. Most of them have a criminal record. I would never think to lock them in a cell for 23 or more hours a day or do therapy when they are caged and shackled. Neither did I do so when I provided psychiatric care in jails and prisons. I have never been attacked physically in any treatment setting. Perhaps I have been lucky, but I believe mutual trust is necessary for safety as well as meaningful change to occur. I see reciprocal mutuality between patients and staff every day at these two programs, which I almost never saw in California correctional facilities at any level.

CHAPTER 12

Sentence Reform and Other Measures to Keep Addicted and Mentally Ill People Out of Jail

———

IN THE FINAL CHAPTERS OF this book, I will discuss how to deal with the interwoven problems of criminalization of mentally ill and addicted people, and overflowing prisons, which have been taking over American society like rapidly spreading metastatic cancers. I will describe ways to keep these individuals out of prison, including sentencing reform, alternative treatments while incarcerated, a system of aftercare that prevents revolving-door recidivism, and decriminalization of so many of these persons who don't belong in prisons. As we shall see in this chapter, there are many different and successful ways this can be accomplished. There are no secret treatments waiting to be discovered. We have many systems that have been proven to work. The *secret* is only that we must address the problem in a multisystemic way that includes all of the modalities I have mentioned.

Liberalizing sentencing would lower the numbers of the incarcerated. It would directly, but nowhere near completely, favorably alter prison environments. In February 2014, the prestigious, bipartisan and independent Little Hoover Commission called for California's leaders to "begin evidence-based reforms to reduce prison overcrowding, reduce recidivism, and prevent crime." The Hoover Commission stated, as did many prison reformers, that 2014 represented *a moment of opportunity* to restructure our sentencing policies.

Though the commission recognized the importance of realignment, it emphasized that this would not affect how long a person is imprisoned; it would only change the place where time is served. The needs of the mentally ill are as poorly served in county and city jails as they are in state prisons. In fact, mental-health care in most local jails is even worse than in prisons.

Although California reduced its prison population by thirty-nine thousand inmates from 2007 to 2014, it did so mainly by transferring prisoners to cheaper, out-of-state facilities and local jails, which themselves became rapidly overcrowded. The state had allocated $1.7 billion to local communities to expand jails by over nine thousands beds to alleviate overcrowding. I would propose at least nine thousand more local mental-health beds, which would do much more to relieve the pressure on jails and prisons as well as better serve the needs of the mentally ill than jail expansion.

Fortunately, some sentencing reforms have taken place in recent years. In his 2014-2015 budget, Governor Brown proposed a process whereby offenders who are sixty or older and have served a minimum of twenty-five years could be eligible for parole.

The courts have ordered the state to establish a parole process for nonviolent second strikers, allowing those who have served half their sentence to become eligible for parole. Proposition 36, adopted in 2012, resulted in the early release of 1,300 offenders in 2013 who were guilty of nonviolent third-strike violations, plus 1,000 to 1,500 more in 2014. The case of William described in a proceeding chapter demonstrates how tedious, expensive, and difficult this process is, but Prop. 36 reform is a way to lower prison populations in a careful, systematic manner.

Governor Brown recommended requiring most felony sentences resulting in county jail time to be split between incarceration and supervision. The *L.A. Times* and many politicians have repeatedly called for more split sentences and fewer correctional beds. In split sentencing, the defendant is ordered to a specific jail term followed by post-release mandatory supervision instead of extended incarceration. This would provide a reentry process with opportunities for treatment, education, and job training. This will not be successful unless there is carefully supervised probation with smaller caseloads and expansion of rehabilitation activities. To accomplish this, funds will have to be shifted from building and staffing prisons to community programs (See Proposition 47 in following chapter).

In a September 2015 op-ed piece in *The New York Times*, David Brooks made the interesting point that the most overlooked aspect of mass incarceration might well be aggressive prosecutors trying to make a name for themselves as tough-on-crime when they run for public office. Under California's Senate Bill 260, which took effect on Jan. 1, 2014, 6,500 prisoners sentenced to lengthy prison terms before they turned 18 will have the opportunity to be reviewed by the Board of Parole Hearings.

While emptying the bucket of prisoners via early release and the above measures, California was still filling it at the other end. In 2012-2013, second-strike admissions increased by 33 percent over the previous year. The state predicts that without sentencing reform, the overall prison population will continue to rise by several thousand yearly through 2019. It will only take a few more murders by former inmates to incite an outcry from a fragile, frightened public, and the pendulum will swing away from all types of early-release programs.

On January 28, 2016, Governor Brown continued his efforts on sentencing reform by proposing that inmates convicted of nonviolent crimes be given a chance at early release. The following day the *L.A. Times* reported that this measure would not result in "droves of inmates winning their freedom" and could make it more difficult for prosecutors to negotiate plea bargains.

In California, 95 percent of criminal cases are resolved by plea-bargaining, another unfair aspect of our criminal justice system. Three or four charges are tacked on to the simplest crime, and then the offender is offered a choice between pleading guilty to a short sentence or a jury trial on four consecutive longer sentences. And so our constitutional right to a trial by a jury of our peers is constantly violated.

The California Penal Code acknowledges that building and operating more prisons is not a sustainable solution. With this in mind, the Little Hoover Commission has made many viable suggestions for sentencing reform. These include not doubling sentences for second strikes and removing burglary from the list of serious and violent crimes. The commission emphasizes the importance of shifting criminal justice resources to community-based programs, including education, supervision, restorative justice, vocational training, work release, substance abuse and mental-health treatment, and comprehensive residential programs.

It clearly states that punishing criminals will not enhance public safety without education and rehabilitation.

The Little Hoover Commission offered Contra Costa County as a model for California. This county's rate of incarceration, parole, and probation is half the statewide average despite the inclusion of cities like crime-ridden Richmond. Contra Costa has lowered the three-year recidivism rate to 20 percent, compared to a state average of over 60 percent.

The county accomplished these goals by:

a. Sending only 13 percent of felony offenders to prison
b. Splitting 89 percent of sentences
c. Cutting probation periods from five years to two to three years

The Commission also recommended reform of drug laws. These include:

d. Reducing the penalty for possession of drugs for personal use to a misdemeanor

e. Reducing penalty extensions for prior drug convictions and lower-level drug-trade workers

f. Allowing all nonviolent drug possession offenders to qualify for diversion

g. Exempting all nonviolent drug felonies from three-strikes life sentences

The Vera Institute of Justice has repeatedly challenged the punishment by imprisonment-only theory and suggests substitution of "appropriate assessments and targeted interventions." The Vera 2013 study, "Recalibrating Justice," interjected a note of optimism about sentence reform. It reported that thirty-five states had passed eighty-five bills reversing the tough-on-crime policies of past decades. The institute believes lawmakers are realizing that carefully chosen community programs can produce better results at lesser cost than incarceration.

Delancey Street is a renowned alternative to incarceration. The average client enters the program with an eighteen-year history of hard-core drug addiction. The program motto is "Enter with a history, leave with a future." The organization has successfully turned around the lives of thousands of ex-felons since 1971. It emphasizes teaching personal skills, and then vocational and educational skills. Delancey Street manages several successful businesses nationally, including restaurants, a catering company, and a moving company.

Homeboy Industries is another example of a program successfully working with gang members and other high-risk youth to prevent behaviors that lead to incarceration. Homeboy offers legal services, tattoo removal, education, and employment in a variety of businesses. These include bakeries, restaurants, farmers markets, catering, silk-screening, and sales of clothing and books. Homeboys has helped one hundred twenty thousand gang members start over. Jorja Leap, a UCLA professor, tracked Homeboy clients for five years. The majority of the three-hundred gang members she followed stayed out of prison, found work, and reestablished family ties. Despite its success, Homeboy continues to receive less than 2 percent of funding from government agencies.

American society desperately needs more programs like Delancey Street, Homeboy Industries, Phoenix House, and Fountain House, where addicts, gang members and the mentally ill can turn their lives around before incarceration or before recidivism becomes a way of life. These programs are excellent in part because they cross over and through prevention, incarceration, and aftercare or probation.

CHAPTER 13

Successful Alternative Treatments in Prison and After Release

———◆———

PENAL AUTHORITIES ABANDONED THE THEORY of rehabilitation in criminology in the 1970s and have not yet developed a theoretical basis for alternatives. Existing practices are a hodgepodge of theories of punishment with little regard for treatment.

The following studies and programs show there is no need to reinvent the wheel. A multitude of programs offers proven, successful rehabilitation and decreased recidivism. They just need to be adequately funded for a sustained period to make a difference.

The Washington State Institute for Public Policy, as cited in the Hoover Commission report, has found several components of cost-effective prison programs with a better than 99 percent chance of being successful. These include:

a. Education
b. Intensive residential drug treatment
c. Outpatient non-intensive drug treatments
d. Cognitive behavioral therapy for high- and moderate-risk offenders
e. Alternative sentences for drug offenders
f. Employment training and job assistance in the community (best begun before release)

These six components for successful rehabilitation in prisons are patently obvious and are cited by many of the successful programs described below. Extensive research has repeatedly demonstrated the success of these programs, yet they haven't been implemented. Why not? Does society continue to need to see the concreteness of overcrowded prison structures rather than community alternatives? Is the need for punishment still so great that it defeats measures of rehabilitation? Is the pendulum swinging back from mass incarceration? Did the 2016 election decide which direction we will take over the next four—or eight—years?

I have evaluated several viable options for successful rehabilitation within correctional settings based on partnerships with private organizations, particularly those that use the following principles: therapeutic communities; accessible religion; and recovering personnel who have successfully survived their own battles with addiction, mental illness, and/or incarceration. Many of these workable programs start within the prisons and provide wraparound services upon release.

A. AMITY FOUNDATION

Amity Foundation offers education and nine thousand treatment beds within California prisons, plus post-release centers providing therapy, transitional housing, education, and family reunification. National Institute of Drug Abuse researchers found a one-year recidivism rate of only 8 percent, compared to a control group with 50 percent return to custody. Five-year recidivism was 40 percent, compared to over 80 percent for the control group.

B. THERAPEUTIC COMMUNITY

The Therapeutic Community (TC) is a modality widely used within prison and jail walls in this country. According to Mitch Rosenthal, the founder of Phoenix House, the TC is capable of "fostering extraordinary changes in attitude and behavior . . . personality, and character." A basic principal is self-help, which includes the following principles:

   a. Active involvement in one's own treatment
   b. Honesty and self-revelation
      a. Acceptance of confrontation as an effective means to achieve the above
      b. Right living with individual responsibility
      c. Extensive use of counselors who have stable sobriety as a result of their own TC experience

The Therapeutic Community fits well into prisons because of its tight, full structure and daily schedule of work, treatment, and education. To be most successful, the TC needs to be separate from the general prison population and continue after release from incarceration. A Vera Institute of Justice study of Phoenix House's Drug Treatment Alternative to Prison (DTAP) program in New York found a 15 percent recidivism rate, with no violent crime.

c. Stay'n OUT

The Stay'n OUT program, a TC based on the Phoenix House model, operated in New York state corrections for twelve years. An external evaluation showed the program was effective in reducing recidivism. New Start, a Phoenix House program in the Orange County, California, jail system demonstrated significantly lower recidivism rates over three successive follow-ups. This program ended when the space it occupied was taken over by a federal reimbursement program for undocumented immigrants. Gateway and Daytop Village have also run several successful TCs in prisons, mainly for inmates with histories of addiction.

D. HOMEBOY INDUSTRIES

Homeboy Industries, like Amity House and Phoenix House, assists individuals released from incarceration as well as those in custody. Most successful programs offer a continuum of care through prevention, intervention during incarceration, and follow-through after release.

Homeboy's motto is "Nothing stops a bullet like a job." UCLA researchers studied Homeboy's 18-month job training and wraparound program for released felons and found its cost and four-year recidivism rate were half the normal rate.

We also need Homeboy-like facilities for the mentally ill, offering structured employment and other appropriate services to maintain these individuals in the community.

Homeboy has saved Los Angeles County and state corrections millions of dollars yearly for 16 years.

Yet government agencies repeatedly withdraw their funds, and the organization has been close to bankruptcy several times. Greg Boyle, the charismatic founder and continuing leader, attributes Homeboy's funding problems to the unpopularity of helping gang members and felons.

E. *GUIDING RAGE INTO POWER (GRIP)*

I first learned about the Guiding Rage Into Power (GRIP) program from my wife, Karen Redding. She met a graduate of the program at San Quentin State Prison during a Spirit Rock, California, retreat to train advanced teachers of meditation. She sensed he was different from the other participants, yet was struck by how rapidly his initial restlessness quieted down.

The GRIP program uses a process known as Insight-Out. The process guides inmates to heal themselves through tools aimed at understanding and stopping violent actions, enhancing emotional intelligence, cultivating mindfulness, and recognizing the impact criminal behavior has on victims. GRIP is easier to sell to prison authorities than many other programs because of its emphasis on controlling anger, an emotion that can be catastrophic inside these institutions.

Jacques Verduin, the director of GRIP, has developed a one-year curriculum now being used at six state prisons. As of summer 2015, Thirty-four graduates of this program had been released over the preceding three-and-one-half years. None has returned to prison, and many have become change agents who work with high-risk youth and prison inmates. One hundred forty-nine graduates were still in prison and helping to turn around the violent prison culture. Insight-Out receives no funding from CDCR and had a waiting list in July 2015 of 476 inmates. GRIP, Amity, Homeboy, and the TCs are all examples of excellent in-house programs that also provide aftercare during probation and parole, and have low recidivism rates.

F. RESTORATIVE JUSTICE

The Centre for Justice and Reconciliation offers an interesting and morally sound solution that focuses on the needs of both victims and offenders, instead of punishing the offender.

Offenses are considered violations against an individual or community rather than against the state. Victims take an active role in the process, and offenders take responsibility for their actions in order to repair the harm they have done. In prisons, restorative justice helps rehabilitation and reintegration into society. Earlier research showed modest reductions in recidivism, but more recent findings show meaningful reductions in the return to crime. This is not surprising, since most in-house prison programs take several years to be effective. The principles of rehabilitation in this method include:

* Victim offender mediation/reconciliation
* Inclusion of families and networks of both parties
* Restorative conferencing to address consequences and restitution while being victim-sensitive (A conference facilitator leads the process.)
* Cognitive-behavioral therapy is used to encourage positive action

J. Latessa has directed over 100 studies of corrections programs at all levels of care. He summarizes his studies in the article, "What Works in Reducing Recidivism?" He emphasizes the importance of evidence-based practices. He firmly states that well-designed programs that meet certain conditions can appreciably reduce recidivism rates for offenders. The basic principles he has empirically validated include:

- Reserve intensive intervention programs for high-risk offenders.
- Do not place low-risk offenders in highly structured programs.
- Target crime-producing characteristics like antisocial attitudes, substance abuse, lack of problem-solving, and lack of self-control.
- Focus on improving attitudes about behaviors, peers, and work.
- Focus on temperament and deficiencies in skills.
- Target multiple deficiencies because high-risk-for-relapse offenders have many risk factors.
- Behavioral programs are most effective. They replace antisocial behavior with pro-social skills and are action-oriented.
- Staff should be well-trained and interpersonally sensitive.

G. FOUNTAIN HOUSE

Fountain House in New York City is a near equivalent of Homeboy for psychiatric patients. It offers a broad spectrum of employment and other appropriate services to maintain these patients in the community. Fountain House places 133 students a semester in academic settings. The organization individualizes the needs of the client and employee, and provides a continuum of support ranging from referrals to job training, on-site support, and absence coverage.

I recall my delight decades ago at seeing patients working beside their social workers in New York City coffee shops. Fountain House states on its website that corporate partners who employ their workers gain enthusiastic and well-trained employees, reduced costs in benefits, recruitment and training and social satisfaction.

H. MEDICARE AND DISABILITY

Many county and state programs are bringing affordable care to medically and mentally ill inmates by using Medicaid under the Affordable Health Care Act. The state of Michigan, for example, anticipates saving $19 million and reducing recidivism through better health care.

SOAR (SSI/SSDI Outreach, Access, and Recovery) is an innovative approach in Miami that diverts the severe mentally ill from prisons to community services. This program is successful in getting 94 percent of applicants onto Social Security Disability Income (SSDI) or Supplemental Security Income (SSI) in less than a month. This is an amazing feat, given that six months or more is my usual experience in helping my outpatients obtain SSDI. These sources provide funds for community treatment and housing, rendering incarceration unnecessary. This diversion program has recently been expanded to released prisoners.

I have found probation and parole effective in helping resistant psychiatric patients and substance abusers adhere to workable treatment. The problem is that these departments are often understaffed, with caseloads exceeding mandated limits. Once again society chooses to prioritize building and staffing tangible assets—such as more prison buildings—over preventing recidivism, despite evidence-based studies.

As previously mentioned, we will undoubtedly need to revive and revitalize the concept of the state hospitals and begin to provide fifty beds per one hundred thousand people in the United States, or about one hundred thousand new psychiatric beds. But we need to reinvent the care given in these new facilities, as well as those dealing with the current fifty thousand state hospital patients. In 1961, the year of my rotation at Rockland State, there were over nine thousand patients and two thousand staff at this mega-psychiatric hospital. This massive model, typical of state hospitals I worked in or evaluated, is more economical than smaller institutions but tends to discourage a therapeutic environment.

A workable cap on numbers of patients would be five hundred or fewer. This is also a cap I would recommend for prisons and jails. Smaller facilities lead to advantages in team cohesiveness and more humanizing contact where staff and patients at all levels are familiar with each other. Ideally, these units would be located close to patients' families, transitional housing, retraining, and jobs.

The American Psychiatric Association [APA] agrees that smaller prisons and mental-health units are preferable. They recommend one full-time psychiatrist for every150 to 200 inmates on medication and one for every 50 inmates in any prison program with a dedicated mental-health unit. The APA also emphasizes the importance of a partnership between mental-health workers and police, courts, jails, prisons, and parole at all levels. The Association calls its recommended system Sequential Intercept, which emphasizes the continuity of care I have described throughout this book.

Mental-health courts and drug courts are another proven way to minimize incarceration and recidivism. They are also referred to as collaborative or problem-solving courts. These courts examine issues in drug- and alcohol-dependent persons, the mentally ill, veterans, juveniles, and the homeless. They involve active judicial monitoring, and a team approach to decision-making involving mental-health providers and probation.

As of 2014, Orange County, California, has nine such specialty courts, which appear to be stretched beyond capacity. They resolve minor infractions and facilitate treatment, through drug and alcohol testing, rebuilding family ties, and providing links to supportive services. Those who do not comply are given sanctions ranging from writing an essay to incarceration. A broad study of four mental-health courts in California, Minnesota, and Indiana showed lower arrest rates and fewer days in jail when individuals participate in these programs compared with a group using traditional measures. I was pleasantly surprised to find there are three thousand four hundred drug courts in the United States.

They are most successful when they can offer sanctions to those who do not comply with treatment and rewards—like removal of jail terms—for those who complete treatment.

The basic requirement for a drug court to work is the ability to provide a continuum of treatment and rehabilitation services.

Recent movements within the community are designed to correct the evaporation of mental-health care. One of these is Connect 4 Mental Health, launched with a 2013 community collaboration summit in Washington DC in 2013. This group facilitates collaboration between all community-based organizations to support the mentally ill. The national Stepping Up Initiative calls on county governments to develop plans with measurable outcomes to reduce incarceration of the mentally ill.

Many new psychiatric treatments have developed in the five decades since the number of state hospitals began to shrink. Current medications are much more effective than older versions and have fewer side effects. They can now be easily tailored to an individual's genetic makeup and metabolic pathways with a simple saliva DNA test.

New, long-acting intramuscular antipsychotic meds currently in use remain effective for two to four weeks after each injection. The FDA approved an injectable form of the antipsychotic iloperidone, which achieves therapeutic levels lasting three months, in summer 2015. This would be helpful for patients who are known not to take their medications regularly.

Cognitive behavioral therapy can be taught more consistently and quickly than other method that had been used previously and has proved more effective with hospitalized patients than traditional talk therapies. Therapy with the families of the chronic mentally ill has recently been successfully tailored to family needs like problem- solving and de-escalation of reactivity.

No single program works for everyone, and some only work for selected populations. One universal element of success is continuity, in which the same team follows an inmate from sentencing through incarceration, pre-release, and aftercare. When this system is impossible to implement, there needs to be other means of providing connection between the systems through a case manager or careful communication. We do not need to reinvent the wheel. We just need to implement the proven best-practice programs for each individual and keep them going, regardless of politics.

CHAPTER 14

A Way Out of Criminalization for the Mentally Ill and Addicted

———————

THE SUCCESSFUL COLEMAN SUIT HAS begun to improve conditions in California state prisons, although it has not addressed issues of prevention, alternative sentencing or aftercare. A key issue in Coleman has been overcrowding, and as a result of several successful legal actions against CDCR, the inmate population has been substantially reduced. Nevertheless, all three state prisons I visited in 2013 were still extremely overcrowded at the time of my evaluation. Some of the overcrowding was said to be temporary, but this has been a much-repeated excuse for many anti-therapeutic practices over the 25 years I have been evaluating California correctional facilities.

The reduction in the state prison population has led to overflowing local jails, and probation and parole departments with skyrocketing caseloads. This has been termed the Realignment Crisis, and some conservative politicians view AB109, the 2011 law mandating realignment (reducing the number of inmates), as a grave threat to society. Others see it as an opportunity to reevaluate the entire California criminal justice system and search for creative solutions based on evidence-based practices.

Without these solutions, mentally ill inmates flow from state prisons to overcrowded community jails. Private, for-profit penal institutions do not seem a solution, surrounded as they are by as much if not more publicity about deplorable conditions as their governmental counterparts. In August 2016, The US Department of Justice announced it would phase out private federal prisons, declaring them less safe and less secure than governmental ones.

The law firm that employed me as an expert in Coleman is now calling for federal oversight of several county jails. In October 2014, the US Department of Justice took control over Los Angeles County jails because the violent conditions there made inmates more suicidal and mentally disturbed, issues that had not been resolved despite twelve years of federal monitoring.

Actions like these may help solve the severe problems in some county jails but do not approach the major underlying problems. The mentally ill continue to fill local jails, where they generally receive even worse treatment than in state prisons. Lowering state prison populations allows California corrections to provide more humane treatment to the many who remain, should prison authorities be so inclined. However, in my analysis the reduction in population has not resulted in a more therapeutic environment. It is a poor overall substitute for sentencing reform and thorough community treatment.

Progressively unavailable psychiatric care for the severely mentally ill outside of prisons continues to result in an increase in absolute numbers of the incarcerated mentally ill. Even more drastic, though not unexpected, the percentage of inmates who are psychiatrically ill has increased exponentially over these past few decades.

In any treatise on prison and mental-health reform, one is obligated to at least mention the needed changes in our society, which are so critical if we are to get to the root of the problem. Most of the individuals in our prisons are poor, uneducated, addicted to drugs and/or alcohol, and of color. African-Americans represent 13 percent of the US population and use drugs at the same rate as whites, yet they total 40 percent of those incarcerated for drug offenses. They are being punished for their skin color as well as behavior that has its origins in their social, educational, and environmental existence. They did not choose to be born in their drug- and crime-ridden ghettos, and few escape them. I agree with fellow Coleman expert Craig Haney that attacking social and economic inequalities—the reason so many poor people of all races fill our prisons and other public facilities—is as essential as developing "fair, effective, and humane approaches to crime control."

Several philosophical differences between crucial factions seem as irresolvable as conflicts between Israel and Palestine or Sunnis and Shiites. These include conflicts between:

- Mental-health and correctional interests
- The powerful California Correctional Peace Officers Association and prison reformers, including social activist attorneys
- State hospitals that deal with inmate patients and correctional facilities
- Academic departments of psychiatry and corrections. Academic psychiatry holds great promise for resolving many of the problems of psychiatric hospitals and prisons but all too often hesitates to deal with corrections because of elitist attitudes about working with criminals and the need for excessive reimbursement for services.

Perhaps skilled negotiators—rather than politicians, attorneys and judges—could help solve these problems. The severely mentally ill would benefit immeasurably if personal agendas could be put aside and replaced by concern for their well-being.

A June 2014 article in *The New Yorker* by Ruth Margalit emphasized how the popular Netflix show *Orange is the New Black* has increased community consciousness about the problems with our jails. The New York Civil Liberties Union used the show to create positive change in the Riverhead Correctional Facility in Suffolk, New York, where the show is filmed, with a campaign called "Humanity Is the New Black." Although the TV show glamorizes jails compared with my experiences, Margalit's article and the show itself have helped call attention to the plight of prisoners in this country.

We need an adequate continuum of care to treat individuals before they evolve to out-of-control, paranoid, manic, or violent states of mind. President Kennedy's multimodal community mental health center (CMHC) movement provided a lot of good care before it was defunded. One problem with this focus was an overemphasis on keeping sick patients out of hospital beds, which led to insufficient beds for the severely ill and inadequate facilities to prevent those who were temporarily stable from decompensating.

Other problems with the CMHCs were a poorly understood notion of prevention of psychosis and giving a low priority to providing services to the chronic mentally ill. By the time Reagan fully defunded the community mental health movement, sick patients had nowhere to turn. There was little or no inpatient care and no support for public outpatient treatment.

Most importantly, we need early intervention and longitudinal care for the severely ill. A team of mental-health workers should provide this care. Though perhaps idealistic, an effective model for this team would follow the patient and provide services even when he or she is in a psychiatric hospital, in jail, or is homeless. This continuity of care would do much to prevent incarceration as well as provide excellent care during all types of institutionalization.

Many individuals who have a long-term psychosis are too ill to know they require medication. Most of these patients are not dangerous to themselves or others when medicated. Unfortunately, when they are not taking their psychotropic meds, they can be at risk for suicide or violence.

A mechanism is needed so these patients can receive involuntary medications, such as long-acting antipsychotic injections lasting up to one month or more. One such means is Kendra's law, enacted in New York State in 1999 and revised in 2005. This law provides for a complete treatment plan constructed by an examining physician. The patient's need for this level of treatment is assessed in a court hearing.

This plan includes assisted outpatient treatment (AOT) by a mental-health team as well as medications. Treatment must be the least restrictive alternative, but failure to comply may lead to involuntary hospitalization. Kendra's law also applies to individuals who are leaving hospitals or correctional facilities.

Utilizing this law to bring these patients to effective therapy can do a great deal to reduce behaviors resulting in repeated hospitalizations and incarcerations.

The successful results of AOT in New York demonstrated:

* Homelessness decreased by 74 percent.
* Psychiatric hospitalization decreased by 77 percent.
* Hospital stays were shortened by 28 days.
* Arrests decreased 83 percent.
* Incarceration decreased 87 percent.

Patients in New York's AOT said the program gave them control over their lives, made them more likely to keep appointments and take medication, and helped them get well and stay well.

Arizona, Hawaii, Iowa, and North Carolina have also had successful assisted outpatient experiences.

Laura's Law, passed in California in 2002, mandates AOT for the mentally ill. But California gave each county the choice of enacting this law. Few counties chose to do so in the first decade after passage. In 2015, Orange County, California, appropriated $6.1 million yearly ($4.4 million of this from the state Mental Health Services Act) to fund 120 slots of assisted outpatient treatment but without involuntary meds.

In my opinion, 120 slots are far too few to make a dent in the revolving-door problem in that county, since Orange County has lost 800 local psychiatric beds in the past 20 years without an increase in community services. Still, effective treatment can persuade needy individuals to agree to be medicated without coercion.

In its first year of operation, AOT received 422 referrals, and 299 were found to be ineligible. One hundred twenty-three accepted voluntary treatment, and only eight required court-ordered AOT. I hope this will be viewed as a pilot program that will be expanded if successful to eventually meet the mental-health needs of the severely ill in Orange County.

San Francisco voted to enact a similar law in July 2014 and San Diego County in April 2015. Prior to the passing its law, San Diego had an in-home outreach team, which had been successful in engaging over 43 percent of potential Laura's Law cases.

By the end of 2015, Los Angeles County had opened five psychiatric urgent-care centers to deal with psychiatric emergencies. In 2016, Orange County also planned to open several psychiatric urgent-care centers. The pendulum may be swinging back to treating mentally ill individuals who are too sick to realize they need help. They are the ones most likely to be incarcerated.

One example of the difficulties in using available funds for mental-health treatment is the California Mental Health Services Act, passed in 2004. The act placed a 1 percent tax on incomes over $1 million to be used for new mental-health treatment and prevention. This act currently generates $1.5 billion yearly, a good portion of which is being saved or redirected by many counties. For example, San Diego County had $170 million unspent and Orange County $220 million by the end of 2015. There is also considerable evidence that counties all over this country are diverting or saving funds raised for mental-health purposes or unwilling to meet requirements for matching funds. I find this unbelievable given all the recent publicity urging adequate mental-health care as a solution to criminalization of the mentally ill.

Proposition 47, approved by over 58 percent of voters on the November 2014 ballot in California, was a good test of where California stands on this issue. This bill was seductively entitled The Safe Neighborhoods and Schools Act. The basics of this proposition were to lower prison populations by sentencing reforms, such as reclassifying personal drug possession from a felony to a misdemeanor. This proposition was expected to reduce forty thousand felonies to misdemeanors and make seven thousand inmates eligible to apply for early release. The theft of property valued at less than $950 was also changed to a misdemeanor. Funds saved by eliminating long prison sentences were to be used for mental health, drug rehabilitation, victim services, and to reduce the number of school dropouts.

However, it will take years before the considerable savings generated by Prop. 47 can be diverted to community programs. These services must be provided sooner and effectively, or Prop. 47 will be labeled another failed attempt at reform.

One unanticipated effect of Prop. 47 was that many drug-related offenders became less motivated to enter and complete rehabilitation when their offenses were reduced from felonies to misdemeanors.

Police officers in California often fail to arrest drug offenders since Prop. 47 passed because they fear there will be no consequences from misdemeanor charges. There are no resources to mandate alternative treatments, as there were when drug offenses were felonies.

In January 2016 I attended a meeting with three Orange County community outreach officers to discuss the effects of Prop. 47. Each one cited rising petty crime and drug abuse related to Prop. 47.

They bemoaned the lack of leverage to get suffering addicts "who walk the streets like zombies" into treatment. They can only write tickets and not arrest users of heroin, cocaine, and methamphetamine. They agreed that the overburdened district attorney's office was too busy to press charges for drug problems that would provide more impetus for treatment.

One officer protested that Orange County's liberal interpretation of involuntary commitment kept him from hospitalizing seriously ill mental patients, particularly when they had no health insurance. The county supervisor who chaired the meeting agreed there was a shortage of psychiatric beds and other services for the mentally ill and addicted who are roaming the streets as a result of Prop. 47. The officer said promised services had not been implemented but by then the supervisor had begun a plan to establish psychiatric urgent care centers throughout the county by 2017.

My son was on his way home from college for Christmas vacation in 2014. Every one of his worldly possessions was in his car. He stopped in Ventura for a surf contest and headed for his car after his first heat. He was shocked. In that short time his car with his lifetime accumulation of worldly goods was gone from its nearby parking place.

Ten days later the car was found in Ventura. The woman driver and all four male passengers had outstanding warrants for methamphetamine-related charges. The driver was placed in a local jail awaiting sentencing for 100 days. She was released back to probation, without any referral to treatment. This deeply angered my son, who—despite his own work on prison reform and his fiercely liberal politics—thought she deserved a lot more punishment.

L.A. County Sheriff's Department narcotic arrests decreased 48 percent in the first five months after the proposition went into effect. Firefighters were among those opposing release of these inmates; they lamented the loss of the most competent workers on their inmate fire crew. Other Prop. 47 antagonists immediately pointed to tragedies like three trick-or-treaters in 2014 that were run down and killed on Halloween by a drunken driver in Santa Ana, California. The driver had multiple offenses and was given many chances at rehabilitation, none of which appeared to be successful.

Property crime surged in Los Angeles after twelve years of steady decline, and Mayor Garcetti named Prop. 47 as one of the factors responsible for the increase. This is another possible result of releasing inmates without developing adequate community programs, but Prop. 47 will be scapegoated for any negative changes in criminal behavior.

One extremely important aspect of Prop. 47 is a section that permits former inmates who've served their time to reduce felony convictions to misdemeanors. As of June 2015, L.A. County had received over sixty-five hundred applications for reducing a previous felony. There may be over three hundred thousand individuals in California who could file to reduce their felonies to misdemeanors. This reduction could go a long way toward helping these individuals become more employable, but removing a felony requires paying attorneys to file and already overworked courts to review appeals.

Although I am philosophically in favor of decriminalizing drug use, I am strongly in favor of rehabilitative, affordable alternatives to incarceration for all drug abusers. I fear releasing massive numbers of inmates without viable alternatives could lead to more

Halloween-like tragedies and possibly another sentencing rebound. Therefore, these programs must be put in place immediately, even before actual savings are generated. The fact that alternative treatments are not available may very well doom to failure another well-intentioned effort at sentencing reform.

Opponents of prison and sentencing reform include the extremely powerful California Correctional Peace Officers Association and many towns in central California whose fiscal livelihood depends on jails. For example, the town of Adelanto, facing a $2.6 million deficit, has proposed a 3,264-bed jail that would not only bring in jobs, but increase local tax revenue considerably.

Comprehensive prerelease is another essential program that must be developed if Prop. 47 is to succeed. This was not a part of the proposition that was initially approved. The months prior to an inmate's release must be used to plan family reunification, housing, employment, mental-health services, and job placement. The lack of prerelease planning and community availability of resources could also doom Prop. 47.

The Helping Families in Mental Health Crisis Act was first introduced by psychologist/ Congressman Tim Murphy (R-Pa.) in the US House of Representatives in 2013. This bill proposed to:

- Permit mental-health workers to provide crucial information to families
- Pay for acute-care psychiatric beds through Medicaid
- Create a new position of Assistant Secretary of Mental Health to coordinate federal programs and mandate evidence-based treatment
- Expand court-ordered assisted outpatient treatment
- Broaden the range of reimbursed psychiatric meds
- Expand mental-health courts
- Utilize evidence-based treatment methods

In 2015, Murphy broadened this bill to give a block grant to states that had an AOT law and double the grant to states that also have inpatient commitment that includes a need-for-treatment standard for hospital admission. Murphy gained support for his bill from American psychiatrists by supporting the parity of mental health with medical conditions and a boost in the psychiatric workforce. A similar bill, The Mental Health Reform Act of 2015, was introduced in the Senate in August 2015 and reintroduced in 2016.

Another piece of legislation, the Comprehensive Justice and Mental Health Act, was introduced in the Senate in April 2015. This bill proposed the promising model of "sequential intercept." This called for using a series of targeted strategies that included specific options for dealing with the mentally ill offender through each stage of the criminal justice system—from arrest through probation, parole, and thereafter. As previously mentioned, this system also calls for partnerships at all levels.

President Obama signed a version of these bills, the 21st Century Cures Act, into law on December 14, 2016. This bill included most of the features in the Murphy proposal as well as grant programs to battle the drug crisis and decriminalize individuals with mental illness.

Many inmates who spend decades in prison develop a multitude of serious medical and psychiatric problems. The elderly population in jails and prisons is increasing more rapidly than the mentally ill, doubling in the past five years. Inmates age 55 and older have health-care costs two to eight times those of younger convicts. This problem is still another reason for general policies of sentencing reform, including medical parole for elderly, non-dangerous inmates.

Hillary Clinton, shortly after announcing her candidacy for president in April 2015, gave a speech on criminal justice reform at Columbia University. Clinton renounced the tough-on-crime policies of her husband's administration. She championed reforms to reduce the numbers of prisoners, provide alternatives to imprisonment for nonviolent drug crimes, and offer more support for mental-health treatment. Issues of mass incarceration and criminalization of the mentally ill had by that time become a major focus of national public interest and a debatable election issue. In November 2015, the *L.A. Times* reported that all major candidates for both parties were proposing significant reforms in criminal justice and mass incarceration, but none had a fully viable program.

Recently, a conservative groundswell toward conservative solutions to this problem has been led by an organization called Right on Crime. Backed by the billionaire Koch brothers, it also embraced presidential candidates Rand Paul, Jeb Bush, Rick Perry, and Ted Cruz. The Kochs are even donating money for legal representation for indigents and cosponsoring conferences with the ACLU on judicial reform. A major motivation of conservatives would be the huge cost savings achieved by reform. However, I must wonder if these savings would be diverted to tax savings rather than to proven alternatives in correctional systems and community programs.

In his January 12, 2016, State of the State address, Chris Christie, then Republican presidential candidate and governor of New Jersey, announced that a state prison would be transformed into a drug-abuse treatment facility for inmates with drug problems. Christie stated, "The victims of addiction deserve treatment, whether they're in the community or they are incarcerated."

In 2015, President Obama was the first president to visit a federal prison while in office. He came out strongly against solitary confinement. Soon after, he declared that nonviolent offenders serving exceptionally long sentences should be considered for release, citing harsh sentencing, particularly of black and Latino males. Thirty-five thousand prisoners applied. Initially, only 46 were released, allegedly because it took a long time to review applications. However, by October 2015, the US Justice Department announced it would begin to release six thousand inmates from federal prisons as a result of Prop 47's new sentencing guidelines. This effort is separate from President Obama granting clemency to a total of 348 prisoners in 2015 and 2016, most of whom were nonviolent drug offenders.

Donald Trump's election as a president who believes in law and order left many unanswered questions about the future of sentencing reform, mass incarceration, and criminalization of the mentally ill and addicted. I find it interesting that the value of stock in the private prison company Correctional Corporation of America rose 47 percent in the first few days after the 2016 election. It will be quite interesting to follow the swing of the pendulum during the Trump administration.

I've explained that many alternatives to mass incarceration and its twin, criminalization of the mentally ill and addicted, already exist. There is no single answer, but there are many viable, proven alternatives, which must be implemented if this problem is to be solved. One missing basic ingredient is the need to fund and staff alternatives to incarceration immediately, and not years from now, when it will be too late to divert savings from alternatives to our prisons.

I have been witness to an exponential shifting of the severely mentally ill from antiquated state hospitals to even more primitive jails and prisons. I have observed atrocities in custodial institutions by frightened and furious officers. I have directed some, and observed more, successful programs in prisons as well as alternatives. In 2016 I have noticed a groundswell of support for alternatives to incarceration coming from every political and governmental aspect of society. Trump's election leads me to question if this groundswell will continue.

CHAPTER 15

Some Survive

———◆———

NORTHBOUND'S TREATMENT PROGRAM HAS A policy of giving awards for dedicated service at a monthly staff meeting. In the summer of 2016, one of the men who drives the residents to their appointments received the award. Sammy, as I will call him, is a big guy with white muttonchops, rosy cheeks and ham-hock arms. He radiates a youthful energy that belies his sixty-five years.

I was intrigued by his brief narrative emphasizing how he had turned his life around after forty years of criminal behavior and incarceration. I interviewed Sammy on five occasions over a two-month period in my office at Northbound. This chapter is about Sammy's survival and his gradual recovery as he described it to me in these sessions. His story is his own version of his journey and as subject to external scrutiny as any memoir.

Sammy wrote the book on juvenile delinquency by the time he was twelve: shoplifting, setting fires, truancy, disrupting classrooms, drinking whiskey, and smoking Pall Malls. But the structure of his life quickly went from teetering to collapse in 1964, when his father suffered a stroke followed by a fatal heart attack when Sammy was thirteen. Sammy began to hate everything and everybody after his father's death. He had already learned to stuff any feelings of vulnerability. He choked up as he described what he felt at the time.

"I struck out any way I could. I became a terror. I was going to teach God and the world a lesson."

I asked Sammy to describe his father and his relationship with him. Sammy was annoyed with himself at how emotional he was becoming but readily reached back into his past and told the story of him and his dad.

"My father was a union rep for the auto workers union, and he and Mom owned two bars. The union was pretty powerful back then. They threw acid on the cars on the lots to get the bosses to let the car salesmen and mechanics unionize.

"He took me to a South Side Chicago barbershop where he conducted his union meetings. I felt so special because I was the only kid there. We also hung out in his bars, which were open all the time except between four and six a.m. All the guys who hung out at the bar used to come to the house a lot. They played pinochle and ping-pong, and placed their bets with Mom and her sister. They'd smoke Chesterfields and Pall Malls, and beer and whiskey were everywhere. Everyone who came to the house knew his or her guns had to go in the kitchen cabinet. I loved to climb up on a kitchen chair and stare at them, yearning to touch the .357 Magnums and .38s."

Tears streamed down his cheeks when he began to reminisce about the good times. "My dad taught me how to play baseball and football. I even scored a touchdown once in Connie Mack football and made the local newspapers—the first and only time I was in the news for something good and not for trouble."

Sammy recalled the life lessons his father taught him about making the right decisions, still surprised at the myriad of emotions he was feeling. "I cut school a lot when I was ten. When my father found out he said simply, 'pick a belt.' I picked a skinny one. It hurt bad, but I wouldn't cry. My older brother taught me to pick the fat Garrison belt because it didn't cut the skin so much. After that whipping I went to school every day till his stroke."

Sammy had an obsession with setting fires until his father caught him. "I poured gasoline in a soda can and was just about to light it when Dad came upon me in the act. He screamed and kicked me in the ass. The shock went straight up my back to the tip of my neck. I stopped playing with matches after that.

"Sundays we'd go to church in the morning, and afterwards we each got a quarter to go see a double feature at the movie theater. I took a few quarters from the donation box when they passed it around. I didn't think anyone saw me. I asked Dad for the quarter. He looked straight at me and said, 'Get the belt.' By then I knew to pick the Garrison."

Sammy respected the many ways his father parented him. "He'd kiss me on the cheek a lot, but when I talked back he'd backhand me in the face. As long as he was alive he nipped my bad stuff in the bud.

"I worried about him a lot after his stroke. I said good night every night and checked that he was still breathing. One night I heard him get up and slosh around in his slippers. He came to my door and said, 'Sammy, get Mom.' Then it all happened so fast. The firemen came to the house and took him away. My mom was hysterical, crying and screaming. My brother put me on his lap and told me my dad had a massive heart attack and was dead. I cried out, 'He didn't say goodbye to me.' " At this point Sammy was struggling to hold back his tears and wondered out loud, "Why does this shit still bother me?"

I supported him in letting his feelings out, reminding him he was no longer the tough kid from the South Side of Chicago who had to stuff all his feelings.

I asked Sammy to talk about his mother. "My mother always protected me.

She let me buy 75-cent model airplanes as long as I didn't tell my dad. She also never informed him when the nuns told her about my mischief. My mom knew all the cops. They came to our house to place their bets with her and her sister. Mom's nickname was 'The Duchess.' The police would come looking for me whenever there was a crime in the neighborhood. She always told the same story. 'Sammy was painting the living room that day.' She gave up that alibi after the police responded with, 'Where do you sit? The paint must be so thick by now there's no room for any furniture.' Despite all her rescuing, my mother never told me she loved me. What she did say, and often was, 'You're no good. If I knew I was dying tomorrow, I'd kill you today.' " Sammy's mom sent him quite a double message, putting him down for his criminal behavior while running her own gambling den.

His mom gave up trying to manage him. When Sammy was 14, she sent him to Boys Town, Nebraska. He ran away after ten days and she took him back, but he was arrested soon thereafter for stealing a car and sent to Audy Home, Cook County's juvenile detention center. Once again she took him back after he spent a few days there.

When Sammy was fifteen the courts took custody away from his mother and gave control to his twenty-five-year-old brother, Ted—whose major qualification was that he was physically stronger than Sammy. However, the first thing his brother did was give him a .357 Magnum. Supposedly, the revolver was to be used to protect Ted when he made his rounds collecting insurance payments. The gun was used by Sammy to further his early criminal behavior.

Sammy was offered a job painting houses but couldn't conceive of doing any kind of "real job." He hung out with a group of Polish young men at the Black Orchard Club on the South Side of Chicago. He gave a gun "to a guy who turned me in," and at sixteen was sent to the Illinois Youth Center at Joliet for thirty days and then the Valley View Detention Boys' School. He ran away from there, but when he arrived home his mother told him she'd rented his room. She called the authorities, who sent him to St. Charles Youth Center for six months. Even at a young age he knew how to serve jail time. He especially knew how to survive with the other inmates.

"The Polish guys and the Hispanics hung out together, so nobody bothered us. I learned, if beaten, don't cry; get a baseball bat. I refused to shovel coal, so they put me in the hole for ten days where there was no light. They'd open my cell door every day and spill a bucket of water on the floor of my cell to wash it out. I had to use my only towel to squeegee the floor, and then dry myself if I was lucky enough to get a shower. They would fold the paper plate of my food in half so all the food got mushed together. I was filled with hatred for the staff when I got out of the hole. The chip on my shoulder was bigger than ever. Still, I always joked and entertained the other inmates. I made them feel good to be with me."

Sammy was released under supervision and forgot he'd left some pot seeds in the pocket of his sweatshirt. The possession of marihuana was considered a probation violation, and he was sent to forestry camp for four months. Two "big time" black street gangs befriended him and taught him to box. His last juvenile facility was named Starved Rock. There he united with his enemies from the street in their mutual struggle against the guards, only to fight each other again when they were all out.

Sammy reported that the guards there put a broomstick inside the Whiffle ball bat, the only instrument they could use to punish the juveniles. He winced when he recalled the pain inflicted when they hit him on the hands with the reinforced Whiffle.

He was out of institutions only briefly, and at the age of eighteen he was sitting on a park bench drinking whiskey when a policeman asked for his license. He gave it up so begrudgingly that the officer challenged him to take it back. They scuffled; he was cuffed and taken to the station, where several policemen hit him in the ribs, he said.

In what Sammy termed his early childish provocation phase, he challenged them with, " 'Take the cuffs off me and we'll see.' They took them off and then they all jumped me. They took special pride in giving me the worst beating of my life, even though or maybe because my mom was their bookie." Sammy broke out with spontaneous laughter at that point and giggled at himself. "I didn't get even one punch in. They really gave it to me."

This scuffle resulted in his being sentenced to three years at Joliet Correctional Center, his first adult prison. His coping strategies failed him there, and he felt he suffered a great deal of "mental damage."

"There were two of us in a one-man cell and 75 on a tier. They sewed all my pants pockets shut. We all shaved with the same razor and top of a grease can for a mirror. Shaving was tough when I was one of the last to use that razor.

"I had the support of the 87th Street Boys. We were Polacks, wops and spics, but we all got along in the prison environment. I refused to work there. I said if I wanted to work, I would have worked on the streets. The guards there must have known my mom because they didn't throw me in the hole for not working.

"I was beginning to figure things out when I had my first visit with my sister. My ankles and wrists were shackled, but it was a taste of home. I returned to the cellblock and looked down at the walkway to nowhere, just cell after cell. I was overcome by loneliness. I felt cold and alone. The guard put me in my cell and closed the cold metal door with a loud, icy clang. The hatred I felt for this prison welled up inside me, but I wasn't ready to begin to change myself."

Sammy only served about half of his time at Joliet and, shortly after he got out, he and his future brother-in-law started scoring and shooting heroin together intravenously. He stopped for a day and thought he had the flu. Suddenly he realized he was addicted and began breaking into houses to support his habit. This sent him in and out of prisons, but his record of bank robberies kept him out of treatment at the Federal Medical Center in Lexington, Kentucky, where he desperately wanted to go. He was not treated for his addiction and psychological problems at any of the prisons he cycled through. He hid his painful emotions and was driven by hatred.

Sammy described his feelings as he told the narrative of his early years in adult prisons. "I'm smiling now. I always smiled. Even then to hide the pain and hurt. Today my smile is full of joy." With that emotional comment, he suddenly found a flood of tears streaming down his face, moistening his puffy sideburns. "Don't worry, Doc, these are happy tears," he said.

At the age of 18 he found a 17-year-old sweetheart. They married and had a child shortly after she turned 18. Her story tells a lot about the social network that surrounded Sammy. "She had seven sisters; five dated ex-cons. One married a Chicago cop, and one worked at the Cook County Jail. I still hung out with the 87th Street Boys. There were fifteen of us, and we'd play ball. If we didn't have a game or there was a long seventh-inning stretch, we'd pull a theft.

"So I was in and out of jail a lot, but we still had another kid. The last time she picked me up at jail I said, 'Jail was tough. I need a vacation.' She stopped the car, stared for a moment and screamed, 'What? I'm taking care of two little boys alone, and you tell me you need a vacation. What about my needs?' I just got out of the car and walked home. That was it for us.

"In 1976, I started robbing banks by myself. I also was playing softball for a team sponsored by my mom's bar. Tom, a guy on the team who I later learned was an informant for the FBI, tried to set me up to rob a bank. He told me there was a $50,000 payroll coming in, so I got my sawed-off shotgun, and he and I stole a Cadillac.

"On our way to the bank I saw a new TV I wanted to buy so badly, I went to the bank twenty minutes earlier than we planned. I went in looking very tough, grabbed the money and ran out, but Tom took off without me. I got out of there twenty minutes before the feds came and hid out in San Francisco, moving to a different hotel every night. But I felt a pull to go back to Chicago, driven by a strange urge I didn't fully understand. I just felt more comfortable there.

"As soon as I got home I went to a methadone program where I always bought drugs. I noticed a bunch of city employees working by a manhole just outside the clinic. Suddenly they flashed their FBI badges, and they arrested me without a struggle. They had me evaluated by a psychologist who interviewed me and gave me an inkblot test. He concluded I was a paranoid schizophrenic with homicidal tendencies. I was given a twenty-year federal prison sentence in Oxford, Wisconsin.

"There were a lot of guys there who had embezzled to pay gambling debts, so my mom knew a lot of them. It was like a resort, but the Klu Klux Klan was very active there. My mom's contact people there who were with organized crime persuaded me not to join the KKK and took care of me. Once again I felt like an important person in the prison. The Mafia told the guards to let me in the kitchen to eat whatever I wanted. I was their errand boy, so I ate well and had notoriety—what the other guys in the joint tried to get for themselves."

Sammy only served a third of his twenty-year sentence since this was before the "War On Crime," escalated, but was quite institutionalized by the time he got out of Oxford. He heard a wooden door slam and didn't know how to react because he'd gotten so used to the sound of metal doors. The forgotten sound of wood on wood actually frightened him so much he prepared himself to fight his way out. He took a train to his halfway house, and when it halted at his stop, he stayed in his seat. "I was waiting for the command 'Get up!' I didn't even know how to get off the elevated train without someone telling me when and how to do it."

In the 1970s his mom introduced him to her boyfriend, Ray. Sammy didn't trust Ray from their first handshake. He was a cab driver who took no fares. He only drove Mafia bosses around town. The Big Boys offered his mom 'the deal of a lifetime'. They proposed to buy her a grocery store. In the back of the store they would set up roulette wheels, craps tables and blackjack. She turned them down, and Sammy hypothesized the Mafia then feared she'd turn them in. She was found strangled to death in May 1977, and Sammy is sure that Ray was ordered to do it. Even Sammy's godfather, who was a vice cop, didn't investigate his mom's death as a murder.

He was able to stay off drugs his first year on parole at the halfway house, but he had made connections with important drug dealers in prison and had plans to become a big-time drug seller himself. He picked up some heroin and gave it to a friend to try. His friend promptly nodded out, so Sammy did some, too. Sammy's face tightened up as he described this big slip. "God, this brings up so much. What a life I lived. I have butterflies in my stomach now."

The next morning, like a scene from *Les Miserables*, a pounding awakened him. He opened the door to find his grimacing parole officer, Mr. M, thrusting a drug screen bottle toward him. He told M, "You don't need it; I'm dirty."

Sammy was assigned to his former cellblock and escorted into his old cell. He was shocked the cell was still vacant, as they were usually filled immediately. The inmates around him asked him if he ever even got out, to which he hesitatingly replied, "I think I was out." He turned toward me and said, "That was my first warning shot from God. It told me I'd be in prison forever." Instead, he was given a two-year parole violation and, with good time, was paroled again in a year.

An old girlfriend found Sammy an apartment right across the street from a bank. His probation officer visited immediately and, of course, questioned the location. Sammy didn't rob the bank, but he started a "chop shop." He obtained a list of needed parts from ten different models of cars and began his search.

He was driving to his first job with a stripper from Kansas City when he spotted a jewelry store and impulsively stole five diamond rings. Shortly after fleeing the robbery, he rammed into a car and the police chased him. He threw the rings in a dumpster before he was arrested but was sentenced to ten months in jail. However, he was released right away because he was the only one in the lineup when he was identified as the robber, which constituted an illegal lineup.

In March of 1989 he visited his sister in L.A. She introduced him to methamphetamine dealers, who gave him a job delivering chemicals and carrying their guns. These dealers took care of him: they bought him fine clothing and gave him strong meth. One day he found the street where he worked cordoned off by police. He told his sister about this and she advised him to get out of town and hide out in treatment. He checked into the Rocque Center in Orange County and went through its ninety-day program with little motivation to do anything but hide from authorities. He knew how to do time in treatment or prison without really changing, so he stayed off illicit drugs without changing his values.

When he was last in jail one of the inmates with a long prison term asked him to check in on his girlfriend. Sammy visited her after he got out and found she was dealing the "strongest uncut meth possible." Sammy was six months clean but injected the drug as soon as he caught a glimpse of it. As high as he was, he was sure he saw a police battering ram just outside the window. He was right. The police charged into the house, where they found meth, $5000, and a cache

Sammy said to the officers, "Take the money and the guns, and we'll forget about it." He and the meth dealer were both arrested, but she told the authorities he was just visiting, so they only gave him thirty days for being "under the influence."

Sammy tried to make a commitment to recovery after he was released, but he lacked the necessary dedication, so he returned to his criminal lifestyle and was sentenced to California's infamous High Desert State Prison for assault. His past was now catching up with him, and he was sentenced to thirty-two months.

In 1996 Sammy began to get serious about sobriety and attended AA meetings. He met an old girlfriend who was twelve years sober by this time and married her. He worked at the Rocque Center but felt the pay was far too low. So even though he helped recovering addicts during the day, he sold illicit drugs at night. He was arrested for possession of stolen Xanax in 2000 and arrested again in 2004, his last arrest. This time he faced his third strike and a seventy-year sentence, but when he was in a holding cell awaiting sentencing he felt a spiritual awakening begin.

"They put me in this crowded cell where everyone was praying. They were holding each other's hands, but the leader puts his hands on my shoulders, looks me in the eyes and says, 'God tells me we have a miracle here today.' I didn't believe him at the time, but when I went into court the DA (district attorney) jumps up in front of the judge and demands, 'He has to do fourteen years!' The judge stares at the DA and says, 'Don't tell me what to do! I'm striking all the strikes. I'm giving him six years with half time off for good behavior.' Then the judge looks at me and says, 'Next time it's twenty-five to life.' "

The door of recovery was beginning to open. His former boss at the Rocque Center visited him in prison. Sammy told him how happy he was to be sentenced to only six years, to which his mentor responded, "I wouldn't give them six seconds." Sammy's head began to clear from the drugs and, as his fog dissipated, he began to accept that the prayers in the holding cell had made a difference. His former boss's words, the prayers, and the threat of twenty-five to life got to him. He learned that his drug-dealing sister and brother-in-law had died. He just didn't fit into prison culture anymore. He was getting older. His knees hurt so much he couldn't run. It was all starting to add up.

He shipped out to a firefighting camp, where he says he was only one of three out of 123 inmates who wasn't doing drugs. He told me he survived only by feeding and talking to the wild turkeys at the camp. "I could never get those turkeys to follow me up the mountain no matter how hard I tried.

"I kept asking to get 423 days of good time restored, and they kept turning me down. One day the captain came up to me and said, 'You've got the days. You leave tonight.' This really hit me. I wasn't ready. I had no plan but to use drugs. Then I thought I could hit someone and they'd put me in the hole, and I'd have time to have my ex-wife pick me up and find a place for me.

"I couldn't decide, so I climbed the mountain to look for a sign from God. I climbed to the top and sensed a presence. I turned around to see the turkeys looking right at me. That was my sign. I choose to leave that night and, somehow, my ex picked me up and took me to the Rocque Center, where I stayed for a week."

A wide smile crossed his face after he told the story of his rescue by the turkeys. "I feel so full of joy now." Suddenly tears welled up and his eyes met mine. "I was a no-feeling guy. If I showed feelings people would take advantage of me. Heroin helped wipe my feelings out. But there were good times then, too. Telling my story helps me remember them."

In 2009, Sammy earned his way off parole, but felt he was still struggling to maintain his sobriety. He had knee surgery and the surgeon gave him Norco (a combination of acetaminophen and hydrocodone) and Oxycontin, to which he quickly became addicted. After a year of pain pills he started on the maintenance blocker Suboxone, which helped him be free of opioids.

He pledged to his sponsor he would lead a decent life and, from then on, each day became easier. His values changed. The man who had refused to work took on two demanding jobs, which he still maintains. He drives the residents at Northbound to their therapy sessions while using his own experience, strength, and hope to guide them. In his other job, he takes care of pets when the owners are out of town and also protects their houses by staying overnight. These are the same sort of houses he broke into for years. I asked him how he felt about being on the other side of things. He responded with another brief narrative about his gradual recovery.

"One Christmas I stole the presents placed by the tree when I broke into houses. The next day I felt so badly about that I decided I'd never rob a house again, and I haven't. I still feel so badly about that. I'm not at all tempted now when I stay in their houses; and besides, they have video surveillance cameras there."

Sammy has health insurance now and has been able to see a psychotherapist. However, he informed me with a chuckle, "I was too much for her, so she sent me to a psychiatrist." The psychiatrist did not prescribe medications but helped him deal with his incomplete mourning of both his mom and dad.

His recent exposure to psychotherapy is probably what helped him be so emotionally revealing to me. I also gave him a copy of my own recently published memoir so he could get a feeling for my personal narrative. He saw many similarities in my beginnings in the ghetto of South Philadelphia to his own Chicago South Side experience. He regretted that his early years could not have been directed in a similar path to mine, but when our paths cross in the halls and driveways of Northbound he laughs about one of my adventures that he read about in my memoir.

Alcoholics Anonymous has been and is essential to Sammy's six-and-a-half years of recovery. His sponsor has stuck by him since 1989 through years of relapses and incarcerations until Sammy "stopped trying, started doing, and accepted decent values," and got sober in March 2010. Sammy now attends four AA meetings weekly, lives the principles of the twelve steps, speaks with his sponsor regularly, has a home group and a commitment as secretary at another meeting. These are all components of a successful program to maintain sobriety and eliminate criminal behavior.

Another important part of Sammy's personal growth was restoring his relationship with his two sons, whom he hadn't seen in two decades. He flew back to Chicago to see them in 2014. He boarded the plane apprehensively. "I was frightened of what I'd feel, what my sons would say. I had a fantasy my sons would beat me up. As soon as they saw me they held me, kissed me on the cheek like my father did to me, and said, 'I love you, Dad.' My God, this solidified me." He continues to communicate with his sons and gleefully shared with them his joy at the Cubs' 2016 World Series win. Even his two college-age grandchildren have visited him and told him they were so happy to have a grandfather.

Sammy concluded his discussion of reunification with his family by saying, "I was in the fear lane when I was by myself. How things have fallen into place. Rarely am I not happy or smiling now."

He concluded our last interview with tears in his eyes, "Doc, I'm such a pussy now for crying, but our talks have really helped me. I'm so much a better man now than I was before I got sober."

Sammy's fascinating story of his criminal past and recovery recapitulates many of the chapters in my book about the past five decades of criminalization of the mentally ill and addicted in contemporary society. His narrative began amid a world of organized crime, which guided him into antisocial activities beginning at a very young age. His delinquent activities were barely kept in check by his father's tough love, but when his dad died an early death, Sammy's anger and grief unleashed a fury of criminal behavior. His early years in juvenile facilities did not include treatment or rehabilitation and only furthered his criminal behavior.

His first adult prison was the overcrowded Joliet facility in a double-booked cellblock. Overcrowding and its damage to mental health were a key issue in the Coleman and Ruiz suits described in preceding chapters. What Sammy mainly learned during this incarceration and the many that followed was hate for authority, how to game the system, how to please and be liked by most people, and how to align with criminal schemes while outside prison walls. He received no treatment for his addiction or mental-health issues.

Then, when he was out and wanted drugs, he went to a methadone maintenance treatment program. This type of program was often underfunded or owned by profiteers. There were few opportunities for necessary ancillary treatments, so they became magnets for active addicts and dealers.

Sammy endured so many years of imprisonment he forgot the sound a wooden door makes or how to sit or stand without a command. This is illustrative of how inmates become so institutionalized they are too crippled to perform the barest tasks of daily living when they leave prisons. Hence the need for programs that teach and mentor necessary skills during and after incarceration. Sammy recovered in spite of his many years in prison, not because of them. And, like many recovering individuals, his road to recovery was through gradual acceptance of a higher power.

He did not have a dramatic spiritual awakening but a series of minor miraculous happenings, which led him to believe in the God he rejected when his father passed away.

EPILOGUE

I SAW MY FIRST CHRONIC mentally ill patient as a sopho-
more medical student in the late 1950s. The chairman
of psychiatry theatrically interviewed a fascinating
group of psychiatric patients from the stage of a large,
packed auditorium on Saturday mornings. Some students even brought dates to the performance. I felt
the demonstration of pathology to be demeaning to
the patients at times, but I kept coming because I was
already considering psychiatry as a career.

The following year I visited my first psychiatric
hospital and made my first attempt at a therapeutic
case study. Three years later in 1962 I detoxified a
heroin addict for the first time in a hospital when at
the time it was illegal to do so in any other setting.
Addicts were already criminalized, and state mental
hospitals were starting to empty by that time.

I have dated the start of criminalization as 1964, the year of the birth of community mental health. This seems to me to be unfair to this movement, as it contained many worthwhile policies for solving the problems of the mentally ill. The Community Mental Health Act just had a few flaws that could have been remedied with adequate funds and contemporary mental-health practices. I was appalled by the lack of treatment for the chronically mentally ill I observed as a student and resident, but these experiences in no way prepared me for my first job as the only psychiatrist in a federal prison. I truly did not enjoy those two years, but the experience qualified me as an expert in corrections. There were few mentally ill inmates there at that time; they were being handled by psychiatric hospitals.

I evaluated many psychiatric hospitals and prisons over the next five decades, but nothing prepared me for watching videos of the cell extractions I have described in this book. I have seen psychiatric patients involuntarily medicated. I have even directly injected antipsychotic meds into the backsides of out-of-control patients. I have also ordered seclusion and restraints for these same patients, taking great pains to remove the devices as soon as the patient regained control. I found many abominable conditions in these facilities, but I never was permitted to observe firsthand the level of brutality I saw in the videos of cell extractions in California correctional facilities.

These involuntary extractions were to me cruel, sickening, and inhumane; yet they were planned, knowingly recorded, and conducted according to established corrections protocols. However, the majority of cell extractions are spontaneous and not recorded. Given the energy of emergencies and the lack of surveillance, we can only assume these unpremeditated procedures are far more barbaric than those that are taped.

The difficulties presented by these seriously ill patients are well known; some have been found guilty of murder. But repeated incarcerations, stays in solitary, forcible extractions, and inadequate care make them worse and worse. The resulting increasing gravity of their illness makes them more and more difficult to treat in the present and progressively more troublesome in the future.

Tales of a Prison Psychiatrist describes the evolution of the problems of mass incarceration from its origins to the emerging solutions of the past few years.

These recent positive measures are emerging from class-action lawsuits, documentaries and other creative social media, judges, courts, legislators, and politicians seeking office. Yet many potentially excellent legislative solutions had not become law as of

December 2016, and most likely similar bills will not pass in the future.

Many alternatives to traditional incarceration have been defunded or dismissed despite their proven success. We do not need to fund studies or pay consultants to come up with new answers. We have many examples of successful prevention, sentencing alternatives, noncustodial treatment programs, and aftercare as well as continuity of care. We have modalities for better treatment of mentally ill and addicted individuals outside of custodial care as well as within the walls of penal institutions.

I would even propose that we resurrect the Community Mental Health Act but correct its fatal flaws. To do this we would need to apply evidence-based models of prevention, reinvent state psychiatric hospitals that are smaller units with modern treatment facilities, fund new programs before we close alternatives, ensure federal and local collaboration, provide long-term continuity of care, and even guarantee funding unencumbered by politics.

Over the past few years we have seen the pendulum swing away from mass incarceration. This movement is occurring not just in the United States, but also all over the world. My greatest fear is that evidence-based programs will not be funded in time to provide necessary care in these alternative, more therapeutic environments, leading to a few horrific crimes by inadequately treated patients. These crimes may then push the pendulum back toward fear-based restrictive settings.

This issue is currently a rare political hotbed in which liberals and some conservatives can come to mutual agreement, albeit for very different reasons. It is time to harness this energy, use the many evidence-based approaches cited in this book in a meaningful manner, and make the changes necessary to reverse mass incarceration – and do so in a way that leads to sustained solutions to a grave problem.

———————

BIBLIOGRAPHY

American Psychiatric Association. *Psychiatric Services in Correctional Facilities, Third Edition.* Arlington, Virginia: American Psychiatric Press, 2016.

Buser, Mary. *Lockdown on Rikers: Shocking Stories of Abuse and Injustice at New York's Notorious Jail.* New York: St. Martin's Press, 2015.

California Dept. of Corrections and Rehabilitation, Corrections Standards Authority, and United States of America. "Security Threat Group Prevention, Identification and Management Strategy." (2012).

Denhof, Michael D., and Caterina G. Spinaris. "Prevalence of Trauma-related Health Conditions in Correctional Officers: A Profile of Michigan

Corrections Organization Members." Desert Waters Correctional Outreach, 2016.

Group for the Advancement of Psychiatry, *People With Mental Illness in the Criminal Justice System: Answering a Cry for Help*: American Psychiatric Press, 2016

Haney, Craig. *Reforming Punishment: Psychological Limits to the Pains of Imprisonment.* Washington, DC: American Psychological Association, 2009.

Hecker v. CDCR. U.S.D.C. (E.D. Cal.), Case No. 2:05-cv-02441-KJM-DAD

Kaufman, E. "Prison: Punishment, Treatment or Deterrent?" *Journal of Psychiatry and Law*, 1(3) (1972): 335-351.

Kaufman, E. "Can Comprehensive Mental Health Care be Provided in an Overcrowded Prison System?" *Journal of Psychiatry and Law*, 1(2) (Summer 1973): 243-262.

Kaufman, E. "The Use of Ex-Addicts and Other Paraprofessionals as Mental Health Workers in Prisons." *Diseases of the Nervous System*, 37(1) (December 1976): 679-678.

Kaufman, E., "The Violation of Psychiatric Standards of Care in Prisons," *American Journal of Psychiatry*, 137(5(1980): 566-570.

Kesey, Ken. *One Flew Over the Cuckoo's Nest*. New York: Penguin Books, 2002.

Commission on California State Government Organization and Economy. *Sensible Sentencing for a Safer California*, 2014

Musto, Davi d F. *The American Disease: Origins of Narcotic Control, Third Edition*. New York: Oxford University Press, 1999.

New York State Office of Mental Health, "Kendra's Law: Final Report on the Status of Assisted Outpatient Treatment." (2005): 2.

Reingle Gonzalez, Jennifer M., and Nadine M. Connell. "Mental health of prisoners: Identifying barriers to mental health treatment and medication continuity." *American Journal of Public Health* 104, no. 12 (2014): 2328-2333.

Rosenblatt, Elihu, ed. *Criminal Injustice: Confronting the Prison Crisis.* Boston: South End Press, 1996.

Simon, Jonathan. *Mass Incarceration on Trial: A Remarkable Court Decision and the Future of Prisons in America.* New York: The New Press, 2014.

Subramanian, Ram, Rebecka Moreno, and Sharyn Broomhead. "Recalibrating Justice: A Review of 2013 State Sentencing and Corrections Trends." *New York: Vera Institute of Justice* (2014).

Torrey, E. Fuller. *American Psychosis: How the Federal Government Destroyed the Mental Illness Treatment System.* New York: Oxford University Press, 2014